AF821354

COMBAT AIRCRAFT

163 MOSQUITO UNITS IN THE FAR EAST

SERIES EDITOR TONY HOLMES

163 COMBAT AIRCRAFT

Jeremy Walsh

MOSQUITO UNITS IN THE FAR EAST

OSPREY PUBLISHING

OSPREY PUBLISHING
Bloomsbury Publishing Plc
Kemp House, Chawley Park, Cumnor Hill, Oxford, OX2 9PH, UK
Bloomsbury Publishing Ireland Limited,
29 Earlsfort Terrace, Dublin 2, D02 AY28, Ireland
1359 Broadway, 12th Floor, New York, NY 10018, USA
E-mail; info@ospreypublishing.com
www.ospreypublishing.com

First published in Great Britain in 2026

A catalogue record for this book is available from the British Library.

ISBN: PB 9781472870704; eBook 9781472870711;
ePDF 9781472870681; XML 9781472870698

26 27 28 29 30 10 9 8 7 6 5 4 3 2 1

Edited by Tony Holmes
Cover Artwork by Gareth Hector
Aircraft Profiles by Janusz Światłoń
Index by Angela Hall
Typeset by Lumina Datamatics Ltd
Printed by Repro India Ltd

MIX
Paper
FSC FSC® C047271

Acknowledgements
The author would like to thank the following sources for their assistance in the compilation of this volume – the Second World War Experience Centre which hosts the Mosquito Aircrew Association archives, the National Archives, the Royal New Zealand Air Force Museum, the Commonwealth Graves Commission, Maj Fred Paradie at the Office of Royal Canadian Air Force History and Heritage, the Battle of Britain London Monument and the de Havilland Museum. The following individuals, primarily the descendants of Mosquito aircrew who flew over Burma, have also provided so much additional insight and some of their personal photographs: Geoff Pridmore, Tom Yanota, Barbara Boon, Richard North, Richard Ewing, Sue Cox, Penny Hunt, Nevin Williams, Matt Poole, Alan Jenkinson, John Kitchen and James Payne (*Through Their Eyes*).

Front Cover
WO 'Benny' Walsh flew his 48th operation during the morning of 26 January 1945. As usual, since setting off for India 16 months earlier, he was flying with Flt Sgt 'Ossie' Orsborn as his navigator. Assigned to No 45 Sqn based at RAF Kumbhirgram, in Assam, they had been allocated Mosquito FB VI HR371 that day. They were one of four crews, led by flight commander Sqn Ldr 'Jock' Torrance, tasked with bombing a suspected petrol dump in the jail area of Fort Dufferin at Mandalay. All the crews were briefed that their 500-lb bombs had an 11-second delay, allowing low-level release.

When they reached Fort Dufferin, the Mosquitos attacked from the east at speeds of 290–380 mph. On WO Walsh's attack, in order to maximise accuracy, he dived down to an altitude of just 600 ft before releasing his four bombs. To his surprise, the weapons exploded beneath their Mosquito, violently rocking the aircraft. The bombs had been dropped perfectly on target, resulting in a huge ball of fire from the exploding petrol dump momentarily engulfing their aircraft. As Walsh dryly recalled, 'At least, as we flew out of the inferno, we knew that the mission had been a success'. With Fort Dufferin in flames behind them, Walsh carefully checked the aircraft's controls for signs of any battle damage and was relieved to discover that there did not seem to be any. Their attack attracted some anti-aircraft fire, but it was not very accurate. Before returning to base, the four aircraft strafed targets of opportunity along the Lashio road towards Nawngkhio, with Walsh shooting up three trucks.

After landing back at Kumbhirgram, Walsh and Orsborn found the tailfin of one of their 500-lb bombs embedded in the fuselage of their aircraft. It had been 'another very close shave'. Walsh was never sure if his aircraft had been fitted with 11-second delayed bombs or ordnance with instant fuses. The squadron had been experiencing problems with the former, resulting in the Operations Record Book noting at the end of the month that 'low-level bombing operations have had to be curtailed due to the doubtful functioning of the 11-second delay fuses. New ones have recently been received, and the squadron will carry out low-level sorties when the target necessitates it' (*Cover artwork by Gareth Hector*)

Previous Pages
RNZAF pilots Sqn Ldr Ira Sutherland and Flt Lt John Buchanan, both from No 110 Sqn, walk in front of Mosquitos believed to have been assigned to No 1672 Conversion Unit at RAF Yelahanka in April 1945. Sutherland was killed on 28 June 1945 flying solo in RF582 near Pauktaw and Buchanan died on 2 May 1945 flying HR446 over Rangoon with war photographer Flt Lt Sidney Woodcock (*RNZAF Official PR5339*)

CONTENTS

CHAPTER ONE
DEVELOPMENT AND TESTING 6

CHAPTER TWO
FERRYING 12

CHAPTER THREE
PHOTO-RECONNAISSANCE 18

CHAPTER FOUR
INTRUDER BUILD-UP 26

CHAPTER FIVE
GROUNDINGS 35

CHAPTER SIX
STRIKE FORCE 42

APPENDICES 93

COLOUR PLATES COMMENTARY 94
INDEX 96

CHAPTER ONE

DEVELOPMENT AND TESTING

The prototype DH 98 Mosquito E0234 at Hatfield in early 1941. Having been commissioned on 12 December 1939, the de Havilland team designed and built this aircraft in record time. The bomber/reconnaissance prototype, it was fitted with Merlin 21 engines and transported by road from Salisbury Hall to Hatfield on 3 November 1940. After being reassembled, the aircraft was rolled out on 19 November and first flown six days later. It was given the RAF serial W4050 shortly after this photograph was taken (*Philip Jarrett Collection*)

The graceful DH 88 Comet, which won the 1934 Mildenhall to Melbourne Air Race, and the DH 91 Albatross airliner were 'proofs of concept' for the company's DH 98 Mosquito. As the threat of war in Europe increased, Geoffrey de Havilland, the founder of the de Havilland Aircraft Company, started conceptualising a 'bomber with fighter speed'. The firm's small design team set about creating estimates for twin-engined Albatross-based designs powered by various engines. With these completed, on 7 July 1938 de Havilland approached the Air Council through Air Marshal Wilfrid Freeman, the Air Member for Development and Production, proposing a bomber of wooden construction, since wood 'is as strong in all but torsion as metal'. His concept was rejected.

Although rebuffed again after the Munich Crisis, with war seemingly inevitable, de Havilland persisted. Through early 1939, the company's team continued advancing the concept of a fast bomber, concluding that all defensive armament could be removed if the aircraft's speed and height performance were sufficient. The Mosquito concept was born!

On 20 September 1939, de Havilland wrote to Freeman;

'We believe we can produce a twin-engine bomber which will have a performance so outstanding that little defensive equipment would be needed. This would employ the well tried out method of construction used in the Comet and the Albatross, and being of wood or composite construction would not encroach on the labour and material used in expanding the RAF.'

One of Britain's aviation pioneers, Geoffrey de Havilland built his first aircraft in 1910. During World War 1 he worked as the chief designer and test pilot for the Aircraft Manufacturing Company. In September 1920 Geoffrey formed the de Havilland Aircraft Company, initially specialising in light biplanes and training aircraft. In 1933 his firm developed the radical streamlined wooden DH 88 Comet monoplane racer, a precursor to the Mosquito (*Philip Jarrett Collection*)

Freeman remained sceptical, but was prepared to meet with de Havilland again. On 12 November 1939, Geoffrey de Havilland and Charles Walker again met with Air Marshal Freeman to argue that removing armament would result in higher speed, hence most interceptions could be avoided. When Freeman asked about the speed, they said that 397 mph was achievable. Since this was faster than the current Spitfire, they were challenged to think about other possible roles the aircraft could fulfil, and a draft requirement was raised calling for a high-speed light reconnaissance bomber capable of 400 mph at 18,000 ft.

At a conference on 12 December 1939, Freeman now championed de Havilland's concept, and the decision was made to order a prototype and a mock-up. Under specification B.1/40, the Mosquito would be an unarmed bomber, although the prototype would be a reconnaissance aircraft.

Detailed design work on the DH 98 Mosquito commenced, and on 1 March 1940, as the development progressed, the Air Ministry placed an order for 50 Mosquitos to replace the Blenheim in the reconnaissance role. In May 1940 the Air Ministry issued specification F.21/40 calling for a fully armed long-range fighter. As a result, de Havilland was authorised to start building a fighter version of the Mosquito.

Both the design and construction of the Mosquito were radical. The composite wood structure, combining lightness with strength, was made of spruce, Canadian birch plywood, Ecuadorean balsa, ash, Douglas fir stringers and walnut, using traditional milk-based casein wood glue to bond pieces together. As well as its innovative composite wood structure, the Mosquito featured drag-reducing ducted radiators, rubber block suspension and interchangeable noses for different variants. Another major manufacturing innovation was the concept of splitting the fuselage down the centreline. Each half fuselage shell was formed from an inner and outer spruce plywood skin sandwiching a balsa wood core with wood formers. Because the two halves were manufactured separately, the internal equipment and services could be installed before they were joined together. The moulds and jigs were designed to facilitate dispersed manufacturing, harnessing the capacity of cabinet makers and carpenters across the country, with much centred around the furniture industry in High Wycombe, Buckinghamshire.

The design and development team worked at break-neck speed on the prototype, designing, manufacturing and testing components to ensure they exceeded the design requirements. The prototype was constructed in one of the barns near Salisbury Hall, Hertfordshire, which had been home to the de Havilland design team from September 1939. By the late autumn of 1940, the prototype was ready to move from Salisbury Hall to de Havilland's Hatfield aerodrome, also in Hertfordshire, for flight testing.

In early November 1940, a few weeks after the Battle of Britain had ended, the Mosquito prototype arrived at Hatfield. Then, on 25 November, Geoffrey de Havilland Jnr, de Havilland's Chief Test Pilot, together with John Walker, the Chief Engine Development Engineer, undertook the first test flight in the prototype, with Geoffrey de Havilland watching. The latter noted, 'The great moment had come after only 11 months from the start of the design of the fastest aeroplane we had ever built – a speed record in itself'.

The test programme progressed quickly, identifying relatively few design changes, the most significant being splitting the flaps and extending the engine nacelles to reduce buffeting on the tailplane. Trials continued, and on 16 January 1941 at Boscombe Down, Wiltshire, the prototype delivered on de Havilland's promise to Freeman – it outpaced the Spitfire, giving birth to the Mosquito legend. The first flights of the aircraft demonstrated its outstanding performance, which immediately overcame any remaining opposition in official circles to its unconventional construction. Government orders started to be placed, initially in limited numbers.

On 15 May 1941, Geoffrey de Havilland persuaded the neighbouring farmer to Salisbury Hall to take down a fence, allowing the second completed prototype (W4052 – the fighter version) to be flown from there to Hatfield. Just a month later, on 16 June, George Gibbins flew the photo-reconnaissance prototype (W4051) out of another adjacent field and on to Hatfield.

Production orders increased rapidly, with Mosquito construction taking place in parallel with development testing. De Havilland had somewhat rashly promised to produce the first batch of 50 bomber and reconnaissance aircraft by December 1941. The company was also convinced that the fighter would be required sooner or later. Sure enough, as flight testing continued, the Air Ministry changed the second order for 150 aircraft exclusively to the fighter variant.

The Mosquito fuselage was fabricated over moulds in two halves, joining along the centreline of the aircraft. This allowed fitting out to both sides before gluing and screwing the fuselage together. However, the Mosquito's wings were fabricated in a single piece. The diagonal spruce wing 'planking' was strengthened for the upper wing surface. The top of the single-piece wing was comprised of three double-skin panels so that it would take compression loads without buckling and failing. Here, a wing surface is being fitted to an internal wing structure in a jig (*Author's Collection*)

Mosquito FB VI HJ719 was the subject of a series of walkaround recognition photographs taken in 1942. The Mosquito FB VI fighter-bomber was developed specifically for intruder strike missions, and it became the most widely used variant. The aircraft was based on the F II day fighter without its air interception radar. The FB VI had formidable firepower, being fitted with four Hispano 20-mm cannon in the front of the bomb-bay, augmented by four Browning 0.303-in. machine guns in the nose. It could also carry two short-fin 500-lb bombs in the rear half of the bomb-bay, as well as additional armament on two hard points under each wing (*Philip Jarrett Collection*)

To facilitate volume production of the Mosquito, de Havilland arranged for distributed manufacturing. The airframe had been designed to allow it to be manufactured by large numbers of companies with no previous experience of aircraft construction. By May 1941, an extensive subcontractor network and supply chain had been established. In June of that year, the Air Ministry increased its order for fighters to 500, produced at 50 per month. In a matter of weeks, this requirement had been increased to 150 Mosquitos per month, manufactured both in Britain and in Canada.

Planning for such an increase was an almost impossible task for the de Havilland team due to ever changing demands. By 8 August, the company had been advised that it should prepare to build 200 aircraft per month. After much pestering from de Havilland, it was finally given a letter from the Air Ministry's Contracts Department confirming the need for 150 aircraft per month, including those built in Canada, which at least enabled the company to place orders for raw materials.

It quickly became clear to the Royal Air Force (RAF) that the Mosquito was a hugely versatile weapons platform – effectively the first multi-role combat aircraft. The Air Ministry soon identified a requirement for a fighter-bomber for intruder strike operations. In 1942, based on the F II day fighter variant, de Havilland started development of the new FB VI, with prototype HJ662 completing its first flight mid-year.

Stripped of the F II's air interception radar, the FB VI retained the type's formidable armament of four Browning 0.303-in. machine guns in the nose and four Hispano 20-mm cannon in the belly. Importantly, in the bomb-bay behind the cannon, it could carry two 500-lb bombs (with cropped fins) and two more under the wings on hard points. Since it operated primarily at low altitude, the FB VI retained the F II's single-stage, two-speed supercharged Rolls-Royce Merlin 21 engines. The FB VI would eventually become the most numerous and widely used Mosquito variant.

HALTING THE JAPANESE ADVANCE

Meanwhile, the war in the Far East with the Japanese was not going well for Britain and its Allies. With the fall of Singapore, Gen Sir Archibald Wavell resumed his position as Commander-in-Chief, India, responsible for the nation's defence. Japanese troops continued their relentless drive, with Rangoon falling into their hands on 9 March 1942.

One of Wavell's concerns was ensuring air superiority. Until this time, Britain had directed many of its Empire forces to assist in Europe and Africa, leaving India dangerously exposed and ill-equipped to see off the Japanese menace with obsolescent aircraft. Recognising that Japan had clear advantages through its extremely capable Mitsubishi A6M Zero-sen and Nakajima Ki-43 'Oscar' fighters, both of which had the range to escort bombers, Wavell asked the Air Ministry for long-range fighters. Critically, such aircraft did not exist.

The only operational British long-range aircraft available in early 1942 were Mosquitos, which were just entering service, and Beaufighters, which were in demand in Europe and the Middle East as interdictors and nightfighters. The Air Ministry informed Air Headquarters (AHQ), India on 21 April 1942 that the Mosquito was experiencing 'teething problems', and 'the need for long-range fighters [for] your command [is] already realised here, and ways and means of providing Beaufighters are being urgently considered in consultation [with the] Admiralty'.

The situation did not improve, with the Imperial Japanese Army (IJA) advancing to the mountain range on the border between Burma and India, threatening India itself. Finally, nearly a year after Wavell's request, in spring 1943, the Air Ministry despatched three Mosquito F IIs to India for weather testing and evaluation. Additionally, even before the first FB VIs had been delivered to squadrons in Britain, de Havilland's development team had been tasked with assessing any modifications for operations in India. The situation in Southeast Asia had become so dire that it had been decided to transfer some of these latest aircraft, together with experienced crews, to India with the hope that the inexorable advance of the IJA might be reversed, or at least halted.

INITIAL EVALUATION

Equipped with Beaufighters from November 1942, No 27 Sqn was an operational low-level intruder unit that had been based at RAF Agartala, about 200 miles northeast of Calcutta, in Assam, from early February 1943. Although Agartala was a busy airfield, it had only one runway – a 5500-ft long all-weather concrete strip, which had a nasty 'roller coaster' dip about 1000 ft from the eastern end. The runway lighting for night operations was provided by 'goose neck' oil lamps. While there was a taxiway running parallel to the runway, there was no parallel 'kutcha strip' for emergency landings.

No 27 Sqn CO, Wg Cdr 'Harry' Daish of the Royal Australian Air Force (RAAF), had been notified in advance of a special detachment to the unit, but had kept the news on a 'need-to-know' basis. Flt Lt David Innes, who was one of the squadron's RAAF Beaufighter pilots, explained;

'Much to the surprise of those at the aerodrome, on the morning of 11 April [1943] a strange aircraft approached and was quickly identified as a de Havilland Mosquito II. DZ695 was to be attached to us for weather trials and operational familiarisation, becoming the first Mosquito sent to the tropics for this purpose. The crew, Flt Lts McCullock and Young, had flown

Mosquito F II DZ695 is seen here almost certainly at Allahabad in early April 1943 following delivery by No 1 Overseas Aircraft Despatch Unit. This was one of the first Mosquitos sent to the Far East for trial purposes, reaching No 27 Sqn at Agartala, arriving on 11 April 1943. The aircraft was written off following an overshot landing at Agartala a little over three weeks later on 3 May (*Author's Collection*)

the aircraft out from the UK. One week later, a second Mosquito arrived, crewed by Flg Off Fielding and Flt Sgt Steer, and on 2 May a third, crewed by Flg Offs Dupee and McDonnell, was attached for the same purpose.'

F G Myers, a representative of de Havilland, was attached to the squadron, whilst Rolls-Royce representative Mr Waterhouse also made a short visit. Both were tasked with monitoring the Mosquitos in the new environment.

Unfortunately, on 3 May, both Fielding and Steer were injured when their Mosquito, having suffered an engine failure, overran the end of Agartala's runway during an emergency single-engined landing. DZ695 was written off and Steer fractured his spine in the crash. Later that month, on 19 May, Flg Offs Dupee and McDonnell completed the first Mosquito intruder operation when they flew into central Burma and attacked a moving train, which was forced to stop. Ten days later, the same crew carried out the second operation, which took the form of a reconnaissance of Imperial Japanese Army Air Force (IJAAF) airfields in the Kanguang, Meikteila, Thedaw and Heho areas. Over Heho they encountered an 'Oscar', but they were able to avoid its attack by exploiting the Mosquito's low-level speed.

In June, an early monsoon disrupted operations. However, the two surviving Mosquitos completed a low-level attack on Kanguang airfield, destroying one aircraft on the ground and damaging two others. Four 'Oscars' were overhead at the time, but they did not attempt to attack the Mosquitos. The weather deteriorated further during their return. To make matters worse, Dupee's aircraft, DZ696, developed a glycol leak in the starboard engine, which he was forced to shut down. Landing at Cox's Bazar, one of his tyres burst, the aircraft became uncontrollable and the port undercarriage collapsed. Luckily, neither crew were injured and DZ696 was repairable.

After two months detached to No 27 Sqn successfully demonstrating the Mosquito's intruding and strike potential, interim reports about the aircraft were sent to AHQ, India. The two surviving Mosquito F IIs and their crews were then transferred to RAF Dum Dum, near Calcutta, for photo-reconnaissance evaluation.

CHAPTER TWO

FERRYING

Mosquito FB VI HJ811 of No 27 Sqn, photographed at Parashuram in February 1944. This aircraft was ferried to India by Flt Sgt 'Benny' Walsh and Sgt 'Ossie' Orsborn, being the first FB VI to arrive in-theatre. Following service with No 27 Sqn, HJ811 was transferred No 45 Sqn in April 1944. Unreliability issues with the aircraft's starboard engine had long plagued HJ811, and these came to a head on 1 May 1944 when an inf ight fire forced its pilot, Australian Flg Off Arthur Huon, to hastily land at the half-completed strip at Rajalmundy, in Tamil Nadu. The aircraft's undercarriage collapsed and the Mosquito was destroyed in the resulting fire (*Author's Collection*)

The specialist RAF unit responsible for ferrying aircraft to the Mediterranean and the Far East was No 301 Ferry Transport Unit (FTU), based at RAF Lyneham, Wiltshire. The first two Mosquito FB VIs destined for India were delivered from Hatfield in early July 1943. HJ787 was handed over to Flt Sgt John Davis and Sgt Richard Goodall for 'acceptance tests', with HJ789 being allocated a few days later to Sgts Albert Goldstone and Cyril Watts.

On 24 July, Davis and Goodall were on an acceptance flight with HJ787 when one of its engines caught fire. Unable to contain the blaze, Davis decided that they had to bail out. Goodall went first, but deployed his parachute too early. It tangled with the aircraft's tail and both crewmen were killed when their Mosquito crashed near Church Stoke Montgomery in Wales.

With this incident still in their minds, Goldstone and Watts set off in HJ789 on their ferry transit to India. On 1 August, they failed to arrive at their next refuelling point. No trace was ever found of them or their aircraft.

In late August 1943, Flt Sgt Sidney Sims and Sgt Harry Randall (an experienced Mosquito crew from No 605 Sqn) arrived at No 301 FTU and were allocated 'factory-fresh' Mosquito HJ812. Nothing was mentioned to them about the fate of the previous aircrews. They started their preparations for their posting to India. Shortly thereafter, Flt Sgt Benjamin 'Benny' Walsh and his navigator, Sgt Harold 'Ossie' Orsborn,

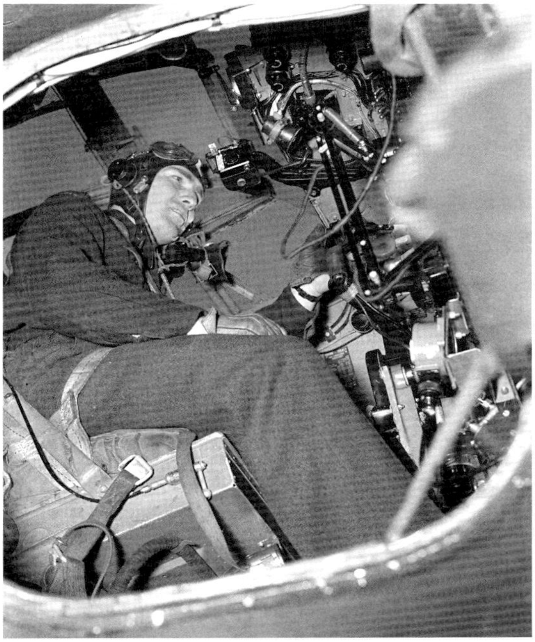

Unlike the Mosquito's bomber and photo-reconnaissance variants, the FB VI, like all fighter versions of the aircraft, had to have its cockpit hatch fitted in the starboard side of the forward fuselage due to the cannon breeches being mounted under the cockpit floor. The cockpit itself was quite cramped, with the navigator sitting a few inches behind the pilot to allow additional shoulder room (*RCAF PL26806*)

arrived at Lyneham, having been posted mid-tour from No 418 Sqn, Royal Canadian Air Force (RCAF). Again, both were operationally experienced 'intruder' aircrew, having flown ops in Boston IIIs before converting to the Mosquito FB VI.

For European operations, the 'standard' Mosquito FB VI was powered by two 1610-hp 27-litre Rolls-Royce Merlin 21s. These 12-cylinder engines were equipped with a single-stage, two-speed supercharger configured to deliver peak performance at lower altitudes. Probably concerned about the effect hotter conditions in the Far East would have on the engines, de Havilland decided to power FB VIs destined for service in India with 1435-hp Rolls-Royce Merlin 23s equipped with a 16-psi boost supercharger. They were also fitted with shrouds to prevent the flare from the engines' ejector exhausts giving away the position of the aircraft at night.

As was standard practice, Walsh and Orsborn were not given a defined route for their ferry flight to India. Further instructions would be given to them on the way to RAF Mauripur, near Karachi, where they would receive details pertaining to their specific postings. Walsh paraphrased his instructions, 'As the authorities said, "Here's a map, get on your way"'.

On 15 September, with auxiliary long-range tanks and loaded ammunition magazines, Walsh and Orsborn flew FB VI HJ811 to RAF Portreath, on the northern Cornish coast. Early the next morning they were briefed on the weather for their first leg to RAF North Front, Gibraltar, crossing the 'hostile' Bay of Biscay, which was routinely patrolled by Luftwaffe aircraft. There were no diversions in case of problems, and Walsh and Orsborn would spend more than four times longer over the water than either of them had previously done.

After taking off, Walsh banked and then flew directly over the airfield so that Orsborn could take an accurate fix for their first leg. He then trimmed the aircraft whilst Orsborn set up his navigation table for the flight ahead, after which they both changed to full 'ops' mode. The latter entailed continuously scanning the horizon for hostile aircraft, interspersed with regular checks on the Mosquito and their route.

Less than halfway through their leg, their Mosquito's starboard engine started to run rough. Walsh and Orsborn were naturally concerned. As the Merlin deteriorated, Walsh decided to shorten the route over water, flying over neutral Spanish territory to get to Gibraltar. Then, if the engine deteriorated further, they at least had the option of either bailing out or force-landing their Mosquito, resulting in them being interned in Spain. Orsborn got to work with his maps to confirm their new heading. Walsh also made the decision to jettison the now-empty auxiliary fuel tanks to reduce drag, after which he concentrated on nursing the ailing aircraft on their new heading directly towards one of the more difficult runways in Europe.

Gibraltar is a peninsular jutting out into the mouth of the Mediterranean. Its most distinctive feature is the huge rock which dominates the territory from every angle and against which its single runway nestles. Once the airfield was in sight, Walsh called the tower at RAF North Front and requested an immediate landing from the northwest. More than five hours after the cliff at Portreath had dropped away from them, he banked his aircraft round in a gentle curving approach towards the runway which jutted out into the Mediterranean. Seconds later, with the starboard Merlin still running rough, Walsh and Orsborn felt relief as the mainwheels of their Mosquito made contact with the runway.

RAF North Front was a busy transit airfield between Britain, the Middle East and India. It was also a key base for the defence of the Western Mediterranean. Walsh was guided to a spot on a packed flightline, where he shut down the Mosquito and handed it over to the groundcrew. Then, he and Orsborn headed to aircraft operations to complete their paperwork. Walsh's declaration that they had been forced to fly over neutral territory was not well received since it required an official apology from the British authorities in Gibraltar to the Spanish. He also reported that he had been forced to ditch their auxiliary fuel tanks, and asked for replacements to be fitted, only to be told that there were none in Gibraltar. Their ferry flight would continue with shorter legs than they had hoped.

On 17 September, Walsh and Orsborn set course for Oujda, French Morocco, with strict instructions to avoid overflying the Melilla promontory, which was part of neutral Spanish Morocco. There, the groundcrew refuelled the Mosquito by 'hand-pumping' from large storage drums. Once this had been completed, Walsh and Orsborn continued eastwards for about 90 minutes along the coastal strip towards Maison Blanche, near Algiers, where they had an overnight stop.

Flt Sgt Benjamin 'Benny' Walsh was only 19 years old, but had already completed 18 intruder operations with No 418 Sqn RCAF, when, having converted from the Boston III to the Mosquito FB VI, he was posted to India. With Sgt Harold 'Ossie' Orsborn, also ex-No 418 Sqn, as his navigator, Walsh ferried HJ811 to India (*Author's Collection*)

The following day, they first flew about 400 miles along the coast to Tunis, where they refuelled. Afterwards, they continued a further 300 miles to Castel Benito, an airfield just to the south of Tripoli. There were still no replacement auxiliary tanks. On 19 September, Walsh and Orsborn flew on for two hours to Marble Arch, a bleak desert refuelling base near Ra's Lanuf in Libya. It was dominated by the Arch of Phila Eni, a huge monument beside the Via Balbia, Libya's main coastal road.

The following morning, they checked out their Mosquito for the 800-mile leg to Cairo. It would be their longest flight without auxiliary fuel tanks, with the first hour across the Mediterranean, followed by a lengthy desert crossing towards Cairo. The navigation would be challenging because, apart from wadis and the occasional oasis, the maps were relatively featureless. They decided to treat the desert leg the same as flying over water.

After more than two hours of flying, when they were in the middle of their desert crossing, the Mosquito's starboard engine started to run rough again. It was the worst possible place for this to happen, since there were no diversions. As they crossed the Qattara Depression, with 150 miles still to go, Walsh had to shut the engine down. He then feathered the propeller, trimmed the Mosquito and flew it for about 40 minutes on only one engine until Cairo appeared out of the haze and dust.

Walsh focused on the potentially tricky single-engined landing ahead, maintaining his approach speed 30 mph higher than usual and only selecting 15 degrees of flap. He lowered his undercarriage and, leaning across to the right, pushed the starboard propeller's 'feathering button'. With the additional drag from the undercarriage and a windmilling propeller, they would not have enough power to overshoot. After more than three-and-a-half hours of flying, Walsh safely landed the ailing Mosquito on a blisteringly hot afternoon.

On 25 September, with the Merlin repaired, Walsh and Orsborn set off for RAF Habbaniya, beside the Euphrates in Iraq. This was another long leg of about 780 miles, but with good navigation fixes for Orsborn along the route. After crossing the Suez Canal near the Great Bitter Lake, they continued across the North Sinai desert heading towards Palestine and the Dead Sea, until they picked up an oil pipeline that was easy to follow east across the desert.

Unfortunately, the starboard engine gave them problems again. This time it lost oil pressure when they still had more than 200 miles to go and were over one of the least-inhabited parts of the Iraqi desert. Walsh shut the Merlin down, retrimmed the Mosquito for asymmetric flight and flew the last hour of the leg on just one engine. By now he was becoming experienced at flying the aircraft in this way. After 3 hr 35 min in the air, Walsh landed the 'rogue' Mosquito safely at RAF Habbaniya.

Whilst the groundcrew started to work on the engine, Walsh and Orsborn reported to the transit centre to sign their aircraft in. They were told that their next stop would be Bahrain. They were also told that Sgt Sims' Mosquito, HJ812, had crashed and burst into flames on take-off from there a few days earlier. Both Sims and Randall had been killed.

On 27 September, with their Mosquito 'rectified', Walsh and Orsborn continued their journey to India. Bahrain was about 650 miles away, and they followed the Euphrates River valley, past Basra on their right-hand side, until they reached the Persian Gulf near to the settlement of Kuwait. They then tracked down the western coast of the Gulf until they reached the island of Bahrain.

The next day, Walsh and Orsborn completed their 'passage to India'. After take-off, they headed east across the northern tip of Qatar and along the Persian Gulf, making landfall on the Arabian Peninsula at the small fishing settlement of Dubai. With the Straits of Hormuz to their north, they flew over the mountain range and then crossed the Gulf of Oman towards RAF Jawaani, on the coast of North West India. It was hot and humid, and the insect life was 'pretty active'. After refuelling, they continued a further 330 miles east, following the coast, to land at Mauripur.

It was only when they signed in that Walsh and Orsborn were told that their Mosquito was the first FB VI to make it to India. However, it was not the end of their journey. The pair remained at Mauripur for almost two weeks, 'kicking their heels' and pressing for information. Eventually, on 10 October, they were instructed to fly HJ811 900 miles across India to RAF Allahabad in Uttar Pradesh. When they arrived, Walsh and Orsborn were separated from their aircraft and given a rail warrant for the three-day journey to the Air Transport Pool at Poona, where they would be allocated to a squadron.

Other crews, who retained their underwing fuel tanks, had less demanding transits to India. Flt Sgt Cliff Emeny of the Royal New Zealander Air Force (RNZAF) and navigator Sgt Johnny Yanota RCAF arrived at No 301 FTU at the end of October 1943. They had a relatively uneventful ferry journey to India with their Mosquito, taking a slightly different route to Walsh and Orsborn, as follows: 11 November – Lyneham to Portreath, 50 minutes; 17 November – Portreath to Gibraltar, 4 hr 15 min; 18 November – Gibraltar to Rabat Sali, one hour; 22 November – Rabat Sali to Castel Benito, 4 hr 40 min; 23 November – Castel Benito to Cairo West, 4 hr 40 min; 26 November – Cairo West to Lydda (near Jerusalem), two hours; and then via Habbinaya, Bahrain, Mauripur and Delhi to Allahabad.

Ferrying new Mosquitos to India would be a continual process. Teething troubles with new aircraft were commonplace, but some 'problems' were more suspicious than others. Most crews ferried the mark that they were intending to fly, although some were eventually posted to learn new roles.

After being awarded his navigator's brevet, Canadian Sgt Johnny Yanota completed the Mosquito conversion course at RAF Grantham, Lincolnshire, where he crewed up with 23-year-old New Zealander Flt Sgt Cliff Emeny. The latter had already completed one operational tour as a gunner, and had recently finished his pilot training. They were then posted to No 60 OTU at RAF High Ercall, Shropshire, for the Night Intruder Course, before being sent to No 301 FTU at the end of October 1943. There, Emeny and Yanota were allocated FB VI HX946 and instructed to ferry it to India (*Tom Yanota Collection*)

After receiving his navigator's brevet, Sgt Alfred 'Alf' Pridmore was posted to No 8 Operational Training Unit (OTU) at RAF Dyce, Aberdeen, to specialise in photographic reconnaissance. There, he was partnered with Flt Lt Richard 'Dick' Campbell RCAF on the Mosquito. Soon afterwards, at RAF Benson, Oxfordshire, the pair were allocated a new Mosquito PR XVI with a pressurised cockpit and double-glazed windows for high-altitude long-range reconnaissance. They ferried it to India for delivery to No 684 Sqn, with their initial reporting point being Karachi.

Campbell and Pridmore took off from RAF Portreath on 26 May 1944, the latter recalling;

'Although we flew the first leg to Rabat at 35,000 ft, we experienced no problems with icing. [The leg] was completed in four hours for 1262 nautical miles, averaging 315 knots, which was not bad for those days. In fact, we took off half-an-hour after two Beaufighters and landed about two hours before them. As we were unable to replenish our oxygen, we finished the rest of the journey to India at lower levels, so no icing problems arose.'

On the next leg to Tripoli, Campbell was feeling rather under the weather following an evening drinking in a bar, so Pridmore, who hardly drank at all, swapped places with him in mid-flight to take over the flying. Changing places inside the cramped cockpit was quite challenging since both men were more than six feet tall. Pridmore continued;

'On our third leg from Tripoli to Cairo we experienced port engine failure due to a loss of coolant and made a single-engined landing at Tobruk.'

All single-engined landings in Mosquitos required skill and concentration. Failure of the port engine added to the challenges facing the pilot on the approach and landing due to the asymmetric torque from

Having completed his nine-month navigation training through to being awarded his brevet, Sgt Alfred 'Alf' Pridmore was posted to No 8 OTU at RAF Dyce, near Aberdeen, to specialise in photographic reconnaissance. At Dyce, he 'crewed up' with Canadian Flt Lt Richard 'Dick' Campbell on the Mosquito. Soon afterwards, at RAF Benson, the pair were allocated a new Mosquito PR XVI and instructed to ferry it to India for delivery to No 684 Sqn (*Geoff Pridmore Collection*)

the starboard engine. Even though Campbell was a relative novice on the type, he executed it perfectly and they handed the aircraft over for repair. 'An astute engineering officer identified the failure as due to possible factory sabotage on the Packard-built Merlin 72/73', Pridmore recalled. 'The leaking coolant pipe had identical punched holes at the upper and lower bends which had been filled and painted over and would eventually leak whichever way the pipe had been fitted to the engine'.

He and Campbell handed over their aircraft to Allied Command South East Asia in India on 6 June 1944.

CHAPTER THREE

PHOTO-RECONNAISSANCE

New Zealander Flt Lt Jack Irvine (right) with an unidentified flight sergeant navigator in front of one of No 684 Sqn's Mosquito PR XVIs being serviced possibly at Dum Dum in early 1944 (*RNZAF Official PR5563*)

In 1943, the photo-reconnaissance tasking in the Far East was the responsibility of No 681 Sqn at Dum Dum. Its eclectic mix of aircraft – Hurricane IIs, Spitfire IVs and Mitchell IIs (ex-Dutch B-25Cs) – reflected its responsibilities covering Burma, China, Assam and the Andaman Islands. Much to the surprise of No 681 Sqn personnel, the two Mosquito F IIs from Agartala landed at Dum Dum on 9 August, crewed as before by Flt Lts McCullock and Young and Flg Offs Dupee and McDonnell. Flg Off Fielding accompanied them. The Mosquitos had been temporarily allocated to the unit for evaluation. However, crews were so impressed with them that, under the guidance of de Havilland representative F G Myers, they were soon equipped with F24 cameras.

On 29 September, Formation Order 512 authorised the establishment of No 684 Sqn, concentrating on the twin-engined long-range photo-reconnaissance role. During October, No 681 Sqn worked through the details towards the official establishment date of 1 November 1943 for No 684 Sqn. The Mitchell IIs, together with five Mosquitos (the two F IIs and three FB VIs), would form the nucleus of the new unit, under the leadership of Sqn Ldr Basil Jones.

On 18 October, the first Mosquito PR IX arrived at Dum Dum. Powered by two-stage, two-speed supercharged Merlin 72 engines, which required an additional 'chin' air intake under the front of the engine cowling, their increased length nudged the spinners in front of the aircraft's nose.

A second PR IX crashed at Ranchi before arriving at Dum Dum, but another arrived on 23 October.

Even though the new unit really needed experienced Mosquito photo-reconnaissance crews, the personnel posted to No 681 Sqn 'made do and learned on the job'. On 21 October, Flt Lt McCullock, accompanied by experienced photo-reconnaissance navigator Sgt Vigers, flew the squadron's first proper operational sortie in a Mosquito when a PR IX went to Rangoon and Magwe. Three days later, this time accompanied by Flt Lt Henry Reeves, McCullock flew to the Andaman Islands to photograph enemy shipping and Imperial Japanese Naval Air Force (IJNAF) flying boat activities. Three Ki-43 'Oscars' tried to intercept them, but they could not catch the high-flying Mosquito. That same day, Flt Sgt Johnson, with Sgt Willis, in one of the modified F IIs, returned safely with photographs of Rangoon, despite another attempted interception by two fighters and anti-aircraft (AA) fire at 27,000 ft.

On 2 November, just one day after its formation, No 684 Sqn recorded its first operational loss. Flg Offs Ernest Angus Fielding and Robert Turton RNZAF set off in camera-equipped F II DZ697 on a sortie to Rangoon. As they returned, they were intercepted by a Ki-43 'Oscar' flown by ace Capt Yasuhiko Kuroe of 64th Sentai. Having damaged the aircraft, he chased them until he saw Fielding 'indicate he could not fight anymore'. Kuroe flew alongside the F II and gestured to the pilot to turn around. Fielding complied, but during the journey the 'Mosquito had much trouble with [one] engine and he indicate[d] he must land'. Kuroe acknowledged and Fielding attempted to land in a small clearing, only to hit trees, lose a wing and explode. Kuroe circled the site until it was clear that neither crew had survived.

Despite this early setback, No 684 Sqn flew 38 Mosquito photo-reconnaissance sorties during November, many of which required refuelling at Feni or Chittagong before continuing south over Burma. During the course of the month, plans were formed to relocate both Nos 681 and 684 Sqns to RAF Comilla in east Bengal, which was significantly closer to Japanese-held territory. The personnel and equipment move would take several days by train, ferry (across the Brahmaputra River) and train again to complete the journey to the railhead for Comilla. Each leg of the trip would take more than 48 hours to complete. The first train departed on 3 December, with No 684 Sqn's relocation completed six days later.

Meanwhile, on 5 December, one of the squadron's PR IXs brought back the first photographs of the notorious Burma–Siam railway being built by Allied prisoners of war. Five days later, Flg Off Eugene Cotton and Flt Sgt Raymond Woods took off in the remaining F II, DZ696, for a sortie photographing the Rangoon area. Once again, Capt Kuroe managed to intercept the Mosquito, pursuing it for 40 minutes over the sea and damaging the aircraft's port engine. Despite his guns jamming, Kuroe used the same tactics and bluffed the crew into turning back to land at Rangoon. Cotton duly flew to Kuroe's airfield in loose formation, at which point the IJNAF pilot indicated that he should land. Unfortunately, DZ696 hit a tree on the approach to the runway and both Cotton and Woods were killed in the resulting crash.

These early losses notwithstanding, the Mosquito was really starting to demonstrate its photo-reconnaissance capabilities. On 15 December, for example, Sqn Ldr Basil Jones, with Flg Off R C Hawson navigating, photographed Bangkok for the first time since the evacuation of Burma. The flight covered 1700 miles, and both men were awarded immediate Distinguished Flying Crosses upon their return. Five days later, Wg Cdr William Moffat Murray arrived from Britain to assume command of the squadron.

Wg Cdr William Moffat Murray (left), the new CO of No 684 Sqn, and New Zealander Flt Lt Cliff Andrews in discussion probably at Dum Dum just after the former's arrival from Britain in December 1943 (*RNZAF Official PR5568*)

On 23 December another Mosquito crew was lost when FB VI HJ760 crashed. Flg Off Alexander Gray Orr RCAF and Flt Sgt Frank Johnson were killed when the aircraft flew into a water tank 20 miles south of RAF Feni. There is a suggestion that this aircraft may have suffered structural failure moments before it hit the tank. Its loss was made good on 29 December with the delivery of PR IX NR464 by Flt Lt 'Koss' Newman and Sgt E K Smith.

During December, No 684 Sqn completed 36 operational sorties in Mosquitos. At year-end it had two Mosquito FB VIs, six Mosquito PR IXs and four Mitchell IIs on its establishment.

January 1944 saw the beginning of an aerial survey of Burma in preparation for its reoccupation. The Mosquitos inevitably flew the longest and most productive sorties, complementing the detailed survey work of No 681 Sqn. The photo-reconnaissance aircraft frequently revisited key places of interest like Port Blair on East Andaman Island, the Burmese cities

Flt Lt Cliff Andrews (right) and an unidentified flight sergeant navigator in the cockpit of a No 684 Sqn Mosquito in early 1944. Andrews (flying with Flt Lt Jack Irvine) later went on to break distance records and also to photograph the summit of Everest (*RNZAF Official PR5561*)

of Rangoon and Moulmein, with the latter's port and railway receiving close attention, further south along the Burma–Siam railway and Bangkok. A 'mosaic' of these important sites was soon created as a result of the numerous missions flown over them.

On 25 January, a movement order was received for No 684 Sqn to return to Dum Dum. Planning and packing started immediately, and three days later the equipment train was loaded and departed for the slow journey back north of Calcutta. The personnel train followed in the early hours of 29 January, with both trains arriving at Dum Dum station on the 31st.

Flying from Dum Dum on 7 February, Sqn Ldr Jones, with Flg Off Hawson, photographed Port Blair and the four flying boats at anchor in its harbour. At 1232 hrs, whilst flying at 34,000 ft five miles north of the port, an IJNAF A6M3 'Hamp' attempted to engage the Mosquito from a distance of 1500 ft below the aircraft. Jones evaded the

LACs I Harris and D Fisher of No 684 Sqn inspect and clean the register glass of an F24 vertical camera fitted to a 14-in. lens on the ramp at Alipore in mid-1944. Once they had completed this job, they would instal the lens and camera into the Mosquito PR XVI behind them (*Public Domain*)

This high-altitude photograph of Port Blair and its airfield on East Andaman Island was taken by Flt Lt F W Guy and Plt Off Gerrald Stevens of No 684 Sqn on a sortie from Cox's Bazar on 27 March 1944 (*Public Domain*)

fighter by opening the Mosquito's throttle, maintaining height and altering course, leaving the 'Hamp' behind.

Later that same day, two crews arrived with new PR IXs, one of which was MM257. Unfortunately, this aircraft did not serve for long because, 11 days later, its pilot, Flg Off Ronald Hodge (with Flg Off Richard Burridge as navigator), became unwell during a sortie to the Andaman Islands, forcing the crew's early return to RAF Ramu. On departing for Dum Dum a short while later, the aircraft swung on take-off, the undercarriage collapsed and the Mosquito was so badly damaged in the subsequent crash it was written off.

AA fire could reach the Mosquitos' operating height, and the CO experienced a barrage when he next visited Port Blair. Despite being accurate for height, it was about two miles behind them. Although AA guns and the threat posed by Japanese fighters were always taken into consideration, they did not prevent the undertaking of operations. Targets obscured by cloud cover, however, routinely caused the rescheduling of sorties.

Over the following months, adding imagery to the survey 'mosaic' continued to be No 684 Sqn's primary tasking, reaching deeper into Japanese-held territory. These long-range high-altitude photo-reconnaissance sorties presented crews with certain challenges, as Flg Off Jack Winship (with Flg Off Peter Haines as his navigator) explained: 'After the fuel tanks were all topped off [in PR IX MM294] at Ramu, we set off for Kaungean [on 5 April], located near the eastern border of Siam, close to the Indochina area.' The aircraft had 50 gallons of fuel in each drop tank, and this would only be needed once 100 gallons from the main tank had been used up.

However, on trying to transfer the fuel between tanks, the crew received a red light on the instrument panel, indicating a vapour lock. Knowing that these often cleared as the temperature cooled, Winship maintained their course for the target at an altitude of 35,000 ft, aided by a 'terrific' 100-mph tailwind. He continued;

'I was ready to try to transfer fuel from the drop tanks once again when I noticed my port engine temperature was climbing. I looked out, and there was this horrendous plume of vapour trailing from the engine – just a colossal cloud. Startled, I realised it was my coolant and immediately shut the engine down, feathering the prop before the Merlin heated up to seize.'

Unfortunately, the port engine also drove the Pesco pumps that transferred the fuel between the tanks. They immediately turned back towards Ramu, some 800 miles away, needing the 100 gallons in the drop tanks to reach the airfield. However, without any functioning Pesco pumps to transfer the fuel, Winship was left with little choice but to jettison them in an effort to reduce drag. Unable to 'hold 35,000 ft on one engine', he 'maintained airspeed by sustaining a slow rate of descent'.

The crew sent out an SOS, without any response. Since the electrical generator was also driven by the port engine, they also needed to conserve battery power. With insufficient fuel to reach Ramu, they considered diverting to China, before discounting that idea. They also contemplated crash-landing onto a riverbed and trying to make their way back on foot. Then, suddenly, their sole Merlin started running rough. Momentary

On 30 May 1945, No 684 Sqn's Sqn Ldr Kossuth 'Koss' Newman and navigator WO Reg Smith completed a record-breaking Mosquito PR 34 flight from Benson to Mauripur in an overall time of 12 hrs 25 min at an average speed of 378 mph. The Mosquito, RG185/Z, which was a standard reconnaissance aircraft, carried full camera equipment. Three other PR 34s that had left Benson a day earlier also made the flight in less than 13 hours *(RNZAF Official PR10081)*

concern evaporated when they realised that its supercharger had cut out with decreasing altitude. According to Winship;

'When the supercharger cut out it was like losing another engine, so I immediately opened the throttle again to retain boost. Finally, with my boost regained, I was able to hold the aircraft on an even keel at around 14,000 ft with no difficulty.'

To reduce drag, he then re-feathered the port propeller, which had been gently windmilling, and flew directly towards Ramu. They overflew the Arakan Yoma mountains at 14,000 ft with an airspeed of 200 mph. With better-than-expected fuel consumption, their optimism increased. The SOS had also been picked up in Calcutta and forwarded to Ramu. 'We still had some petrol in our tanks as we neared Ramu', stated Winship. 'As our Mosquito approached the strip, another Mosquito pilot entering the circuit heard our R/T conversation with the field. He orbited and followed me to make sure I maintained my airspeed coming in on one engine on a fairly short strip'. Winship successfully completed a single-engined landing on Ramu's 'Reindeer 2' airstrip.

The next day, after a faulty coolant hose had been replaced, Winship and Burridge flew the Mosquito back to Dum Dum. All bar the CO congratulated them for bringing the aircraft back – Wg Cdr Moffatt Murray 'tore them off a strip' for not turning back with the vapour lock. Nevertheless, Winship was mentioned in despatches for flying the Mosquito 760 miles on one engine.

DISTANCE RECORDS

In May 1944, No 684 Sqn relocated to Alipore, from where it undertook a series of long-distance flights. Flt Lt Kossuth 'Koss' Newman flew 1903 miles to photograph Car Nicobar, in the Nicobar Islands. Next was Bangkok, when 2000 miles were clocked up. This was followed by sorties to Singapore and its railway network, covering 2028 miles. Finally, a survey flight over Mergui, in Burma, set a new record of 2084 miles. By 30 May, working in concert with No 681 Sqn, the two photo-reconnaissance squadrons had photographed 232,100 square miles of enemy-held territory in preparation for reoccupying it. The Allied advance would rely heavily on No 684 Sqn's survey work, which continued to be undertaken through to year-end.

New aircraft, such as the tropicalised Mosquito PR XVI capable of attaining 415 mph and with a range of 2800 miles, were desperately needed to undertake these taxing flights. As noted in the previous chapter, photo-reconnaissance-trained Flt Lt 'Dick' Campbell and Sgt 'Alf' Pridmore had ferried just such an aircraft to India in June 1944. Having reached their destination, they expected to be posted with their aircraft

Mosquito PR XVI A52-600 of the RAAF's No 87 Sqn is seen at Morotai on 4 August 1945 whilst staging from Coomalie Creek to Labuan. Whilst flying from the airfield on the latter island, this aircraft and A52-604 completed 11 sorties over nearby Borneo in ten days (*Public Domain*)

to No 684 Sqn. However, as Pridmore explained, 'On arrival at Karachi we discovered that 684 were more in need of the aircraft than the crew, and whilst waiting to join the squadron we were posted to No 143 Repair and Salvage Unit (RSU) at Bishnapur as a test crew for repaired Mossies'.

In January 1945 there were 12 Mosquitos on strength with No 684 Sqn at Alipore. With larger wing tanks and refuelling at Cox's Bazar or Akyab, the PR XVI's operational range was extended, enabling the Burma–Siam railway to be photographed regularly. With an F24 forward-facing oblique camera in each wing tank and another in the nose, the aircraft 'would dice the railway line to photograph the results of bombing attacks on bridges and railway cuttings'. With AA fire always a concern, crews would photograph an area and then break away into the surrounding hills, before returning to photograph more features further down the track.

Distance records continued to be broken in the new year. On 21 January 1945, a Mosquito photographed the Mekong River, in Indochina, for the first time. Then, on 22 March, Flt Lt Jack Irvine broke the overall distance record for the PR XVI when he flew 2493 miles to photograph the Bangkok–Singapore railway all the way down to the Malayan border. By the end of the month, No 684 Sqn had completed three-quarters of all the basic survey work required for the advance towards Malaya.

By June, the unit's work was being actively supplemented by the RAAF's No 87 Sqn, formed from Mosquito-equipped No 1 Photographic Reconnaissance Unit RAAF during September 1944. Having converted to the PR XVI and operated from Coomalie Creek in Australia's Northern Territory, a detachment of Mosquitos was briefly based on the Cocos Islands in June 1945, intent on photographing targets in Singapore. The squadron then carried out reconnaissance operations over Java, Balikpapan, Halmahera, Biak and the Philippines.

On 16 June, with the Japanese in full retreat, Sqn Ldr Cliff Andrews and Flt Lt Jack Irvine, both of the RNZAF, took off from Alipore in No 684 Sqn PR XVI NS787 (equipped with 100-gallon auxiliary underwing tanks) on a flight authorised as 'a high-altitude fuel consumption test on a course from Calcutta to Darjeeling and return'. In reality, they

This photograph of Singapore's Changi jail was one of a number taken by Sqn Ldr Cliff Andrews and his navigator, WO H S Painter, on 31 August 1945 prior to their aircraft suffering engine issues that forced them to land at Kallang 24 hours before Allied forces entered the city (*Public Domain*)

intended to photograph Mount Everest. Upon returning from the flight, Andrews reported;

'We made a wide circuit and had a splendid view of the southern slopes of the South Peak, Lhotse and the saddle between Lhotse and Everest. I was so dazzled with this scene of beauty that I think I just kept on circling.'

They photographed the peak for more than 20 minutes, Andrews noting;

'As a final gesture, we decided to fly as close to the very summit as possible. As we approached, we closed in, and when the summit flashed past just above our wingtip it was only about 30 ft away. As we crossed the Northeast Ridge we experienced a terrific wallop from a down draught which took us quite unawares, but we were fortunately well clear. At this sign of impatience from the greatest of all mountains, we bade farewell.'

Despite Japan's surrender on 15 August, No 684 Sqn's photo-reconnaissance operations continued. On 20 August, Flt Lt J R Manners, with WO F A Burley, flew 2620 miles in a Mosquito PR 34 from their forward detachment on the Cocos Islands to Penang Island and Taiping, taking just over nine hours.

Eleven days later, Sqn Ldr Cliff Andrews and his navigator, WO H S Painter, unintentionally entered Singapore one day before Allied forces. Having flown from the Cocos Islands to photograph the city in advance of the Allied occupation forces, their Mosquito suffered a constant-speed drive unit failure with one of its Merlin engines. After Andrews had made a precautionary landing at Kallang, the crew stepped out of their aircraft with some trepidation, even though it was two weeks after the Japanese surrender. Luckily, they were greeted 'with much bowing and scraping' by the Japanese. Andrews was subsequently introduced to the senior RAF officer incarcerated at Changi Prison, who arranged for an RAF engineering team to repair the faulty Merlin. The Japanese then refuelled the Mosquito before it departed for the Cocos Islands.

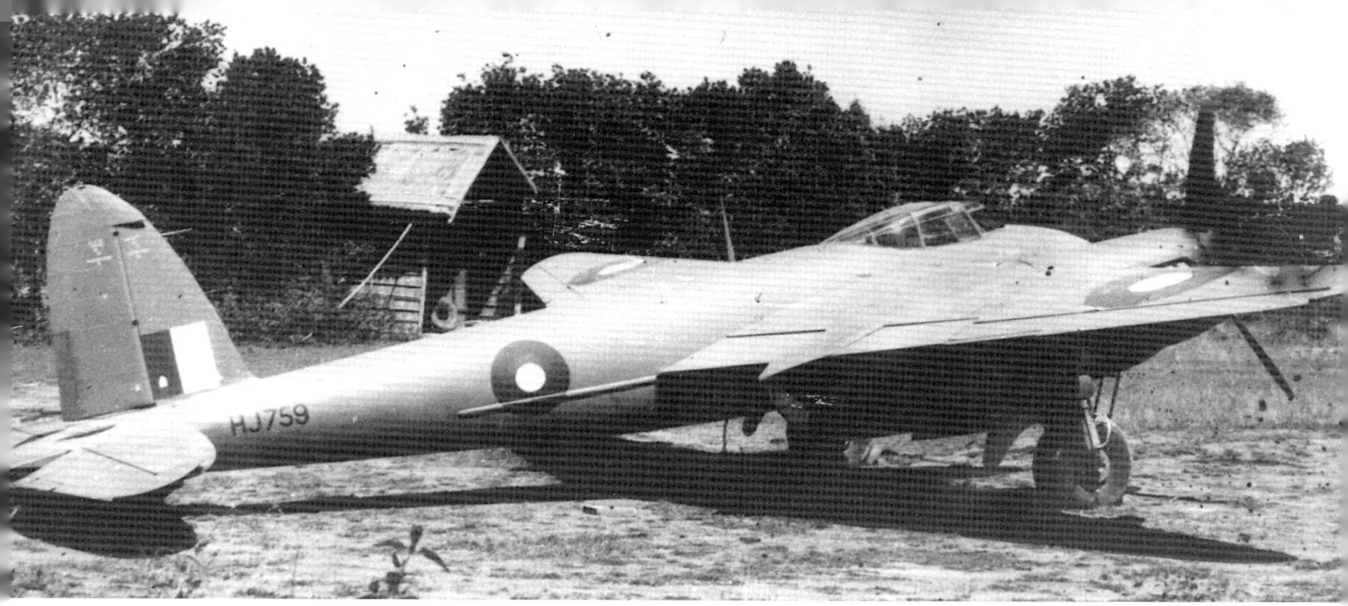

CHAPTER FOUR

INTRUDER BUILD-UP

FB VI HJ759 was one of the Mosquitos delivered to No 27 Sqn in late 1943, the aircraft being seen here shortly after it had arrived in India. This unit operated a mixed force of Mosquito FB VIs and Beaufighter VIFs and Xs for six months until May 1944, when it reverted exclusively to the Beaufighter X (*Philip Jarrett Collection*)

On 4 August 1943, 26-year-old Wg Cdr Eric James Brindley 'Nick' Nicolson was given command of No 27 Sqn. 'Nick', the only RAF Fighter Command pilot to be awarded the Victoria Cross during World War 2, received his decoration for an action on 16 August 1940 during which he suffered serious burns to his hands, as well as other injuries.

Like most intruder units, No 27 Sqn was comprised of two flights, 'A' and 'B', each with ten crews and aircraft and led by a flight commander, plus an aircraft for the squadron commander. In total, there were 42 aircrew assigned to the unit – a mixture of officers and senior NCOs, who worked together. When it came to flying and operations, there was little difference between the officers and NCOs. They did the same jobs and, apart from the CO, knew each other by first names or nicknames.

Nicolson had been tasked with introducing the intruder Mosquito to support the Burma campaign. His plan was to convert 'A' Flight, under Sqn Ldr Ernest 'Bunny' Horn, from the Beaufighter VIF to the Mosquito as soon as examples of the latter aircraft reached the unit. Finally, in late November 1943, four experienced Mosquito intruder crews from No 418 Sqn RCAF (Plt Off Gunn, WO Blinch, Flt Sgts Ball, Rainbow and Walsh and Sgts Luff and Orsborn) were posted to No 27 Sqn, bringing with them the FB VIs that they had ferried to India.

With only four Mosquitos to train all of the unit's Beaufighter pilots, Flt Sgt Ted Ball did most of the initial conversion flights whilst Plt Off William

Wg Cdr 'Nick' Nicolson (seen here as a squadron leader) was the commanding officer of No 27 Sqn at Agartala during the period when it was equipped with both Mosquitos and Beaufighters. He flew one of the first Mosquito FB VI intruder sorties over Burma, on Christmas Day 1943. Sadly, Nicolson was killed on 2 May 1945 when the RAF Liberator in which he was flying as an observer crashed into the Bay of Bengal after suffering an engine fire (*Author's Collection*)

'Billy' Gunn RCAF, WO 'Jackie' Blinch and Flt Sgt 'Benny' Walsh ran the pilot ground school. The pilot conversion training was restricted to just a few flights. First, those converting from the Beaufighter flew in the navigator's seat, with a 'running commentary' explanation from the experienced Mosquito pilot. Then they swapped places. Once conversant with FB VI, they then flew them with an experienced Mosquito navigator, followed by their usual navigator. Concurrently, groundcrews, armourers and engineers were trained on the Mosquito, whilst stores established stocks and their supply chain.

On 16 December, after two weeks of 'working up', the squadron was allocated a special Mosquito task. Sqn Ldr Horn and Flt Sgt Ball, together with their navigators, flew to Ramu. Then, leaving their navigators behind, Horn had the privilege of flying Admiral Lord Louis Mountbatten, Supreme Allied Commander, South East Asia Command (SEAC), on an inspection tour of the Arakan frontlines. Ball flew another 'dignitary'. They were accompanied by Spitfire VCs from No 615 Sqn, and after the tour, they landed their VIPs at Dohazari.

The next day, Flt Lt Alexander 'Jock' Torrance and his navigator, Flt Sgt Jack Shortis, arrived. At 27, Torrance was one of the older pilots sent to No 27 Sqn, having already completed two tours on Hurricanes and Whirlwinds.

At 0645 hrs on Christmas morning, Wg Cdr Nicolson took off on the squadron's first low-level intruder Mosquito operation over Burma. He and his navigator, Flt Lt 'Frankie' Franklin, were accompanied by a second Mosquito flown by Flg Off Thompson and Sgt Chippendale. The two aircraft headed for central Burma, which meant twice crossing the Lushai Hills, Naga Hills or the Arakan Yomas, with some of the peaks exceeding 9000 ft. Electrical storms were very much a part of this hilly region.

They headed for Myingyan, Sagaing and then Thazi, attacking targets of opportunity on the railway and putting a goods locomotive and a tanker out of action south of Thazi. Then, near Yegyo, they attacked a truck, killing some of the occupants. However, the aircraft received some heavy and accurate AA fire when they overflew the IJAAF airfield at Meiktila. After a very successful first Mosquito FB VI operation, both aircraft had landed at Agartala by mid-morning, in time for the officers and senior NCOs to help serve a traditional Christmas dinner to the other ranks.

After more training, on New Year's Eve, Sqn Ldr Horn chose Flt Sgt Ball as his wingman for the squadron's second Mosquito intruder operation, combining expertise and operational area experience on-type, just not in the same aircraft. Both FB VIs returned safely.

The weather at the start of January 1944 was not good. Having flown only four hours in the previous ten weeks, the experienced Mosquito crew of Flt Sgt Walsh and Sgt Orsborn undertook their first operation over Burma on New Year's Day when they flew as wingmen to Sgt Clegg (a converted Beaufighter pilot) and his experienced navigator, Sgt Brinded, who knew the local area well. The two aircraft took off from RAF Agartala at 1345 hrs in the heat of the afternoon for their three-hour operation.

The FB VIs were not equipped with oxygen, so they headed east, aiming for the gap between the Lushai and Naga Hills near Imphal. Then, as they crossed the frontline, they swooped down the eastern side of the Chin Hills towards Kalewa. Constantly scanning for Japanese fighters, they flew at low-level – often less than 50 ft – from Kalewa to Ye-U, looking for targets of opportunity. At Ye-U, they picked up the Irrawaddy railway line and followed it, without finding any targets, towards Monywa, where they banked to the north. Finally, the River Chindwin delivered some targets. Walsh strafed from extreme low-level and claimed hits on nine sampans and a raft, all of which seemed to be loaded with tins. Both aircraft then departed back to Agartala, returning via Imphal.

WO 'Jackie' Blinch, Sgt 'Billy' Gunn and Flt Sgts 'Pop' Ball and 'Benny' Walsh of No 27 Sqn at Agartala in December 1943. They helped other squadron pilots and navigators switch from the Beaufighter to the Mosquito FB VI (*Author's Collection*)

During debriefing, Clegg told the Intelligence Officer that the area had been 'unusually bare of targets'. He had not fired at all. Walsh reported that he completed a single attack – '1 raft, 9 sampans hit with cannon and m/g [machine guns]'.

The squadron's rota alternated between its two flights, so 'A' Flight and its Mosquito crews were tasked with operations every second or third day. On 4 January, WO Blinch, with Sgt Chippendale as his navigator, flew as wingman to Flg Off Cotter. Having attacked two locomotives, Blinch fired at a third one and his Mosquito was caught in the resulting explosion. A large portion of the starboard propeller was blown off, and either this or the explosion itself took the cockpit door off too, slightly injuring both Blinch and Chippendale. The crew shut down the starboard engine and headed north, with Cotter accompanying the damaged aircraft as far as Mombi before continuing to base. Blinch managed to land safely at Tulihal, near Imphal.

A few days later, another Mosquito crew was posted into the squadron, Flt Sgt Johnny Yanota arriving three days before his pilot, the recently commissioned Plt Off Cliff Emeny.

On 12 January No 27 Sqn was tasked with generating a combined Mosquito and Beaufighter four-ship, led by Sqn Ldr Horn, for a night operation to Taungup Pass. Plt Off Gunn and navigator Sgt William Luff were allocated HX946 – the Mosquito ferried out to India by Emeny and Yanota. The aircraft were despatched at roughly 30-minute intervals, starting with Horn at 1750 hrs. He found the target, but because the moon was not up he did not attack.

Gunn and Luff were last seen as they approached the Taungup Pass target at about 2030 hrs, but nothing was heard of them again. One of the Beaufighters returned with engine trouble and the other attacked vehicles in the pass, damaging nine of them. Gunn and Luff were recorded as 'missing, believed killed', having become the first intruder Mosquito aircrew deaths during operations from India.

The experienced Mosquito intruder crew of Flt Sgt 'Benny' Walsh and Sgt Harold 'Ossie' Orsborn stand near one of the bashas at Agartala in December 1943 (*Author's Collection*)

On 24 January, Plt Off Emeny went on his first intruder operation. Paired up with navigator Flt Sgt Yanota, he flew as wingman to Sqn Ldr Horn as both Mosquitos attacked shipping and river communications at Henzada and nearby estuaries. There were 'rich pickings', with hits being recorded on about 50 sampans. At Thabyugyang, they scored hits on a 100-ft black-painted steamer. They then struck a sawmill, brought a lorry to a standstill with cannon rounds and attacked two locomotives. On their return to base, Horn's aircraft suffered mechanical problems, requiring him to fly on a single engine from Buthidaung to Agartala. Even so, it was a very successful operation.

Back in Britain, the Air Ministry decided to re-equip no fewer than 22 bomber and strike squadrons in India with Mosquito FB VIs, replacing Vengeance dive-bombers and some Beaufighters. De Havilland was commissioned to manufacture replacement airframe components in Karachi.

It was now time to extend the Mosquitos' operational reach as far south as Rangoon, and on 3 February, Flt Lt Torrance, navigated by Flt Sgt Shortis, was tasked to lead a 'two-ship' operation to the then Burmese capital. Walsh, with navigator Orsborn, would be his wingman. Both aircraft were fitted with long-range tanks to maximise their range. First they flew south to the airfield at Ramu, near the Japanese frontline, where they topped up their fuel. Soon after departing from Ramu, they were flying low over Japanese-held territory, hugging the western edge of the Arakan Yoma before turning east to pick up the Irrawaddy railway at Henzada. Then, they flew fast and low near the railway, looking for opportune targets to attack. The aircrew called this 'rhubarbing' and it was an important part of most sorties.

Torrance and Walsh continued their search for targets, flying low over Letpandan, Taikkya and Wanetchaung to Dabbin, on the northern outskirts of Rangoon. Following the railway north through Pegu to Nyaunglebin, they attacked a bridge and then headed west towards Prome, where Walsh targeted sampans on the Irrawaddy. The journey home took them through the Taungup Pass and north along the coastal plain, overflying Ramu on their way back to Agartala.

It was a long, exhausting operation, lasting 5 hrs 20 min, with more than four hours spent flying at low-level over hostile territory. On his return, Walsh noted, 'No rail traffic. Bridge at Nyaunglebin shot up. Sampans south of Prome attacked – hits scored'.

On 7 February, No 27 Sqn relocated to RAF Parashuram, 50 miles south of Agartala. Its new airfield lacked night flying equipment, so arrangements were made to conduct such sorties from RAF Feni, ten miles further south. Parashuram's accommodation was quite basic, without local labour being employed to improve it. Within four days, No 27 Sqn's 45 aircrew and 150-strong engineering team had completed the move and operations restarted.

On 12 February, Torrance and Walsh were tasked to fly their Mosquitos even deeper into Japanese-held territory. Walsh flew HX821, again fitted with slipper tanks, for this sortie. Initially heading to Ramu to top up their fuel, they then set off southwards at low level towards Pegu to search for targets of opportunity on the railway between there and Moulmein.

Although neither crew saw any rail movement, there were plenty of targets from which to choose. Having turned to head home, Torrance scored hits on a factory just north of Bilini and then came across a small convoy. Walsh attacked a saloon car with three uniformed occupants, leaving it ablaze. He then strafed three further targets – a three-ton truck, another truck carrying around 30 uniformed men and some bullock carts. Torrance also scored cannon hits on several vehicles, including a bus. Along the river from Kyaikto to Donzayit, Torrance led their attacks on eight 'country craft', including two large ones, and a group of 20 river craft, one of which was left in flames. 'All of the targets were attacked with cannon fire – a total of eight attacks were made, every target being hit'.

By 8 March, the day the pivotal Battle of Imphal commenced, the senior officers at No 27 Sqn assessed the merits of completing the ongoing Mosquito conversion, having flown 45 operational sorties with the aircraft up to then. With the unit about to be 'rested', the conversion stopped. On 13 March, No 45 Sqn, recently arrived at the newly formed No 1672 Mosquito Conversion Flight at RAF Yelehanka, posted four of its Vengeance crews to No 27 Sqn and, in turn, No 27 Sqn posted six experienced Mosquito crews, with their Mosquitos, to No 45 Sqn.

VENGEANCE

Wg Cdr Harley Stumm RAAF, CO of No 45 Sqn, was well respected by his men, the majority of whom were also Australians. Although the unit's aircrew had seen much action flying the US-built Vultee Vengeance I/II dive-bomber from November 1942, the Mosquito FB VI and its intruder mission were new to them when they arrived at Yelahanka, near Bangalore. The unit had a slow start, with the first of its Mosquito FB VIs (LR250), now equipped with more powerful Merlin 25 engines, being delivered on 29 February, with others following. On 13 March, Stumm became the first No 45 Sqn pilot to fly the Mosquito.

The six experienced Mosquito crews supplied to the unit by No 27 Sqn arrived in early April. By then, No 1672 Mosquito Conversion Flight had also received a dual-control Mosquito T III so that pilots, some of whom had never flown a twin-engined aircraft before, could undertake some dual flights before going solo in the FB VI. Most crews had to recalibrate their operational mindset from dive-bombing to low-

Wg Cdr Robert 'Johnny' Walker became CO of No 45 Sqn in May 1944 following the death of Wg Cdr Harley Stumm in a flying accident whilst converting onto the Mosquito. A pre-war fighter pilot, Walker saw action during the Battle of Britain with No 72 Sqn. He was badly wounded during an attack on a bridge over the Sittang River on 25 March 1945 and never returned to operations (*Battle of Britain London Monument*)

level day and night intruder missions. One such individual was Flg Off Walter 'Wal' McLellan RAAF, who had been with No 45 Sqn since it had reformed in November 1942. His views on the Mosquito were very clear;

'A pilot's dream compared to the obsolete Bristol Blenheims and the brutish Vultee Vengeance dive-bombers we had flown before.'

The conversion training was intensive, and in early May No 45 Sqn relocated to RAF Amarda Road to complete a Fighter Refresher Course. Unfortunately, Wg Cdr Stumm was killed, together with navigator Flt Lt Walter McKerracher, when Mosquito HP939 crashed in Calcutta on 13 May. The new commanding officer, Wg Cdr Robert Walker, known universally as 'Johnny' after the whisky, went straight to the squadron's next base at RAF Dalbhumgarh. Here, the unit continued its work up to operational status, crews flying low and at night, but training accidents and casualties continued.

Following a spell in hospital, Flt Sgt Walsh (and Sgt Orsborn) was transferred to No 82 Sqn, which was following a similar conversion path from Vengeances. In August, No 45 Sqn moved to RAF Ranchi for the final stage of its operational training with the Special Low Attack Instruction School. On 13 September, Wg Cdr Walker received the order he had been waiting for;

'SECRET

Movement Order No. 4/44, dated 13th September 1944.

Intention: To move No. 45 Squadron from R.A.F. Station Ranchi to R.A.F. Station Kumbhirgram. Authority H.Q., No. 231 Group Org.

This unidentified No 45 Sqn FB VI ended up in the 'weeds' at Yelahanka during the unit's conversion from the Vengeance I/II to the Mosquito in early 1944. The de Havilland aircraft proved to be something of a handful during take-off and landing for pilots used to the more mild-mannered Vengeance, resulting in sights like this being relatively commonplace. Once in the air, however, the Mosquito was 'a pilot's dream' (*James Payne, Through Their Eyes*)

Instruction No. 21, dated 7/9/44 and H.Q., AC3SEA letter ORG.4/3081 dated 3/9/44.'

Walker accelerated the course completion and arranged for Torrance to leave two days later for RAF Kumbhirgram, in Assam, leading the advance party to prepare for operations. No 45 Sqn would form the core of No 908 Wing, a long-range striking force.

KUMBHIRGRAM

On 28 September, Sqn Ldr Norman Bourke (in HP941) and Flg Off Joe Cartledge RAAF (in HP884) flew to Imphal to take two British Army officers on 'offensive recces' over Burma. They took off at 1515 hrs and headed for the Shwebo area before they split up. Bourke scoured a railway line in the direction of Ye-U from an altitude of 50 ft, attacking a bridge over a canal with two 500-lb bombs fitted with 11-second delay fuses. The weapons fell in the water five yards short and 'no damage was observed'. At Tindeinyan and Chantha, he attacked rolling stock with cannon from 100 ft. Although hits were seen, no damage was recorded.

Meanwhile, Cartledge followed the railway line from Tangon towards Shwebo. At Zigon, he spotted rolling stock, which he attacked from 50 ft with short bursts of cannon, scoring hits. Both pilots, with their army passengers, landed back at Imphal at 1725 hrs. The post-flight report noted 'Recce of special area was completed successfully at heights 2000–2050 ft'.

By month-end, No 45 Sqn's equipment and ground personnel had arrived, but it still did not have a full complement of aircraft. Walker was clearly frustrated;

'Two replacement aircraft arrived today both fitted with Merlin 23 engines and in poor condition, but they were retained because we need machines, and replacements are taking about two weeks to reach us after demand. It is expected that they shall be operationally fit in about three days.'

On 1 October, No 45 Sqn ramped up its operations, despatching ten Mosquitos on three different strike missions. The next day, the unit flew its first night sorties against the IJAAF airfields at Heho and Aungan. Sadly, two days later, one of the two Mosquitos attacking Meiktila and Kangdaung airfields failed to return. Flt Lt Gordon Proctor and Sgt George Bargh (in HP936) were last seen at 1639 hrs near the target on a heading of 300 degrees at an altitude of about 50 ft.

On 4 October, there was an operational stand-down, with crews undertaking training and air tests only. However, during

Although this photograph is of an FB VI being armed at an airfield in England, it clearly reveals the split nature of the mark's bomb-bay and their separate doors. This meant the aircraft could carry two 250-lb bombs, or two 500-lb weapons with cropped fins, in the rear section. The front of the bomb-bay was filled with four 20-mm Hispano cannon and their magazines. The FB VI's four 0.303-in. machine guns, with their magazines, were housed in the nose cone (*Author's Collection*)

one of the latter, 'A' Flight commander Sqn Ldr Bourke was alarmed to see the wing leading edge of his Mosquito starting to buckle as he recovered from a dive. Naturally, he immediately, but cautiously, landed, and the aircraft was transferred to No 143 RSU at Bishnapur for investigation and repair.

Operations resumed on the 6th, with Flg Offs Neil and Hallett despatched to attack Heho airfield. As they arrived, an IJAAF Ki-46 'Dinah' reconnaissance aircraft taxied onto the runway. After a short cannon burst it exploded, allowing No 45 Sqn to record its first aircraft kill. The next day, as operations continued, 'B' Flight commander Sqn Ldr Don Edwards flew to Chiringa, where he suffered a 'vulture strike' during landing. The impact carried away the starboard undercarriage doors and holed the fuselage. Luckily, the aircraft was sufficiently serviceable for Edwards to fly it back to Kumbhirgram, where the damage was repaired. After another rest day, the squadron continued its operational routine, targeting IJAAF airfields and degrading lines of communication whilst coping with daily challenges from their equipment and the hostile environment.

On 12 October, Flt Lt Victor 'Duke' Duclos and his navigator, Flg Off Keith Botterill, led a Mosquito pair on an early morning offensive reconnaissance along the Kin-U railway to the airfield at Meiktila. At 0735 hrs, on their third strafing run on Meiktila in HP833 at just 30 ft, their aircraft was hit on the port side by 13 mm machine gun fire from a Type 93 weapon defending the airfield, gravely wounding Botterill. WOs Wilcock and Maddock in the other aircraft (HP942) immediately took the lead, guiding Duclos in his damaged aircraft towards Tulihal – the closest RAF airfield – near Imphal. Sadly, Botterill succumbed to his wounds during the flight to the base, where he was left behind for burial. The two aircraft arrived back at Kumbhirgram at 1255 hrs. The following morning, Walker, Duclos, Edwards and Flg Off Eric Sandifer flew to Imphal to represent the squadron at Botterill's funeral.

On 14 October, operations were reduced due to preparations for a detachment to Chiringa for Operation *Love*, which required eight Mosquitos and crews to join forces with RAF Thunderbolts in attacks on airfields near Rangoon. On the 16th, the first aircraft of the Mosquito stream took off at 0736 hrs to attack the IJAAF airfield at Zayatkwin, near Rangoon. Taking it in turns to strafe the target, the aircraft damaged a 'Dinah', the airfield control tower, an AA battery and a three-ton truck. On the return leg of the mission they attacked and damaged a factory, a ferry, a sampan and a water tower.

During the attack on the water tower, debris and dust was thrown into the air, with a piece of brick lodging in the starboard engine of Walker's Mosquito. The Merlin failed shortly thereafter, forcing the CO to fly back on one engine to Chiringa. After the successful operation, most of the Mosquitos returned to Kumbhirgram – Torrance and Flt Sgt Ted Rainbow remained at Chiringa until the CO's aircraft was repaired.

That same day, poor weather initially prevented two sorties by Mosquitos at Kumbhirgram. Later, when conditions improved, 'A' Flight commander Sqn Ldr Bourke, with Flg Off Keith Dumas RAAF navigating, took off in HP941, with the second aircraft flown by Flt Lt Arthur Huon RAAF and his navigator, Flt Lt D C MacFadzean.

With the sortie almost finished, Bourke attacked a target near the village of Kadozeik and then pulled up to about 400 ft. His Mosquito was then seen to roll 'to starboard past the vertical and then roll to port, afterwards losing height and the angle of dive increasing as the aircraft approached the ground. It was not actually seen to crash, as trees obscured the view'. Huon circled the area twice but could not see any wreckage, convinced that neither of the crew had survived. Bourke and Dumas were posted as 'Missing, believed killed'. At Kumbhirgram, No 45 Sqn had a 24-hour stand-down, during which time Flt Lt Duclos assumed command of 'A' Flight.

Flt Lt Alexander 'Jock' Torrance, here shown with one of the Mosquito FB VIs of No 27 Sqn in February 1944, later transferred to No 45 Sqn. Door art like that seen here appeared on a number of Mosquitos in-theatre, although it was rarely photographed (*Author's Collection*)

On 20 October, two of No 45 Sqn's Mosquitos were despatched at 0825 hrs on an offensive reconnaissance, but cloud cover forced them to abort. 'B' Flight commander Sqn Ldr Edwards was flying HP921, with Flg Off Sandifer navigating, whilst Flg Offs Neill and Hallett flew HJ291. On returning to Kumbhirgram, both aircraft joined overhead at 2500 ft and 320 mph. HJ291 broke to starboard, and within a few seconds the crew saw what they first thought was a bird falling beneath HP921. Then the Mosquito's port mainplane broke off and the aircraft crashed 650 yards from the runway, 'bursting into flames on impact'. Both Edwards and Sandifer were killed. Walker wrote, 'This came as another saddening blow to the squadron'. Flt Lt Torrance was given command of 'B' Flight.

That same day, a No 82 Sqn Mosquito had crashed following a similar loss of control. Something was definitely not right. All aircraft had to be inspected before flying again. An urgent detailed investigation commenced, since Beaufighter X-equipped No 47 Sqn was starting its Mosquito conversion and Vengeance III/IV-equipped No 110 Sqn would commence its transition to the de Havilland fighter-bomber within weeks.

No 45 Sqn had been flying operations for just over three weeks and had already lost seven of its 42 aircrew. Wg Cdr Walker put out an urgent request for another operational Mosquito crew to be posted to his unit. Having just completed their course with the Special Low Attack Instruction School at Ranchi, Flt Sgt Walsh and Sgt Orsborn were told on 23 October that they were to be attached the next day to No 45 Sqn. By the time they arrived, all Mosquitos on non-operational squadrons had been grounded.

CHAPTER FIVE

GROUNDINGS

Mosquito FB VI HJ770 is seen en route to No 27 Sqn in India in late 1943. Aside from its standard RAF 'Day Fighter' camouflage and markings, the aircraft features the word *SNAKE* above its serial. This was introduced from 1 May 1943 to indicate to units in the Mediterranean that the aircraft must not be diverted to other squadrons whilst en route to the Far East. HJ770 was eventually transferred to No 142 RSU at Agartala and subsequently written off there when a hangar roof collapsed on it during a storm on 5 May 1944 (*Public Domain*)

The Mosquito had been designed by de Havilland to operate as a fast unarmed bomber. Specification 2/40/D.H. issued to the company in 1940 stated that 'the structure must have an ultimate [strength] factor not between 0 and +3.5 g inclusive for the full range of speed up to 450 mph IAS [Indicated Air Speed]'. Due to its outstanding capabilities, the Mosquito was soon modified to perform a variety of other roles that included photo-reconnaissance and operating as a fighter, nightfighter and fighter-bomber.

Minimising weight was essential to delivering the Mosquito's performance. Apart from a slightly stronger 'universal' wing, few significant structural enhancements were made to the airframe across its many variants, although the aircraft's payload and maximum take-off weight slowly increased. Nevertheless, it remained beautifully balanced, with low control column loads – a pilot's dream.

Upon the Mosquito's entry into squadron service, the Ministry of Aircraft Production started monitoring its performance. On 20 November 1942, the RAF's Accident Investigation Branch (AIB) held a meeting for a committee formed to review possible causes for the four Mosquito airframe failures since the type had made its operational debut. Initially, it was believed that there was a possible weakness in the elevators and that the undercarriage doors may have opened during violent manoeuvring.

With de Havilland's assistance, strength tests on the fuselage were completed at Farnborough, Hampshire. Although these trials did not identify any causal link, AIB engineers suspected the undercarriage doors, and recommended tightening the wires closing them. On 25 January 1943, Vernon Brown, the AIB's Chief Inspector, released his report, classified as Secret, in which he recommended that 'before any modification action is put in hand, an attempt should be made to assess the loads on the doors in high-speed flight'.

Six months later, on 14 June 1943, Brown released a report of the second review meeting into the eight structural failures of Mosquitos to that date. They had determined that the failures fell into two classes – the three accidents in which a wing or wings had failed in up-load, the others where the wing had failed in down-load and, finally, where there was no wing failure. The report commented that 'the factor of safety originally considered suitable for nightfighters may now be inadequate', and possibly some of its operational roles ought to be reconsidered. The committee recommended that metal-covered elevators should be used and undercarriage modifications were a priority.

Three more structural failures were considered before the committee met again, with its report issued on 25 October 1943. Working with the Royal Aircraft Establishment, it had reviewed the Mosquito's factor of safety and concluded that there were no compelling reasons to reassess the aircraft's load factor. The report included comments on the way the aircraft was flown since 'although the Mosquito is not classified as "fully aerobatic", it is undoubtedly so treated by many of those who fly it. Moreover, it is perhaps unfortunate that "test" pilots are amongst the worst offenders in this respect in that they set an example to the RAF'.

The committee continued monitoring the Mosquito. By the time the next meeting's report was issued on 25 February 1944, the committee was focusing on wing failure;

'The failure of the airframe structure in four of the five accidents dealt with in this report could be attributed to high accelerations, and the evidence suggested that in each case a wing or wings failed first during the pull-out. The start of the trouble was loss of control, and it is becoming increasingly clear that even experienced pilots cannot afford to lose control in a Mosquito, since on recovery from an out-of-control dive it is all too easy to break the wings.'

FIRST SIGNS

On 13 May 1944, No 45 Sqn's CO, Wg Cdr Harley Stumm, had just completed practising 'quarter attacks' in his Mosquito (HP939) against a USAAF B-25 Mitchell, capturing it on cine film. As he approached Armada Road airfield at about 200 mph at 3600 ft with the Mitchell and another Mosquito, Stumm appeared to lose control of his aircraft. It rolled and dived between the other two machines in a near vertical spin. Then pieces of the aircraft broke off in mid-air, before it crashed into the ground. Both Stumm and his navigator, Flt Lt Walter McKerracher RAAF, died on impact. Within days, the inquiry into the failure of HP939's airframe attributed it to the undercarriage doors having come open during sustained high-g.

In London on 27 August, the AIB issued another report about the Mosquito. It had reviewed ten structural failures that had occurred between April and

On 13 September 1944, FB VI HP886 of No 82 Sqn 'crashed unaccountably' whilst carrying out high-g quarter turns and attacks on another aircraft at a height of 5000 ft during training near Mysore. Flg Off William 'Tuffy' Tufnell and Flt Sgt Victor Abel were both killed (*Author's Collection*)

June 1944. Although it was not included in its review, the AIB referred to Stumm's failure in India, despite its information being both incomplete and, in places, incorrect;

'In addition to the accidents which occurred in this country, a few details are available concerning a similar occurrence in India. The aircraft, No. H.P.939, which was probably a P.R. Mk. IX or a P.R. Mk. XVI [it was an FB VI], broke up during a rapid recovery from a dive after the pilot had carried out an aerobatic manoeuvre at a low altitude. The accident was attributed to over-stressing, but the preliminary report stated that one of the port undercarriage doors flew off and struck the tailplane. Mod. 499 [positive lock on undercarriage doors] was not embodied.'

The panel reviewed the effects of various modifications, most importantly one to strengthen the joint in the main spar;

'Mod. 638 [strengthening of leading-edge skin] Class 2. A retrospective modification introduced to strengthen the bottom wing skin at the bottom boom of the front spar. It was suspected that the butt joint in the skin along the centreline of the spar was conducive to splitting of the boom, and the modification consists of a plywood strip bridging the gap in the skin. One thousand sets of parts have been delivered by 18/6/44.'

The AIB urged that this modification be implemented without delay.

Two weeks later, on 11 September, Flt Lt John Reeves RNZAF, with navigator Flg Off Leonard Prout, lost control of his No 45 Sqn Mosquito (HP915) during evasive action on Random Range. Failing to pull out of a low attack, the aircraft dived straight into the ground and both airmen were killed. Then, within 48 hours, No 82 Sqn Mosquito HP886 'crashed unaccountably' whilst carrying out high-g quarter turns and attacks on another aircraft at an altitude of 5000 ft during training near Mysore. Flg Off William 'Tuffy' Tufnell RAAF and Flt Sgt Victor Abel RAAF were both killed. Witnesses said that Tufnell's Mosquito disappeared beneath the target aircraft, possibly being thrown upside down.

On 10 October, No 45 Sqn Mosquito FB VI HX821, which had been sent to No 143 RSU at Bishnapur for repair, inexplicably broke up in mid-air during an air test – it was believed at the time that the aircraft may have suffered a bird strike. Flt Lt 'Dick' Campbell RCAF and No 143 RSU's Chief Technical Officer Flt Lt Douglas Rimell were killed. Within the tight-knit Mosquito community, concerns were rising. There were rumours of 'wood shrinkage'.

The failures continued. Ten days later, at No 82 Sqn, Flg Off Ronald 'Babe' Wambeek and navigator WO Brian Mooney were scheduled to practise shallow dive-bombing over the range, following on from Flg Offs Al Parker RAAF and Maurice Randall RAAF, who took off just before them. Wambeek stated;

Twenty-one-year-old Canadian pilot Flt Lt Richard 'Dick' Campbell, seen here, and 28-year-old Flt Lt Douglas Rimell, No 143 RSU's Chief Technical Officer, were killed on 10 October 1944 when No 45 Sqn Mosquito FB VI HX821 broke up in mid-air during an air test. The aircraft has been sent to No 143 RSU for repair (*Geoff Pridmore Collection*)

'We never saw them again. While waiting our turn on the bombing range, a telephone message came through from the range officer. Al and Maurice had "gone in". Apparently one wing had disintegrated during the first bombing run, causing the aircraft to roll over and dive into the ground in front of him.'

According to No 82 Sqn rigger Aircraftman Ralph Whitworth;

'Al took off, and on the way to the range the wing came off and the aircraft crashed and burned, with both Al and his navigator being killed. The wing that had fallen off did not burn and was brought back to us.'

Flg Off Arthur Maude, navigator for flight commander Sqn Ldr 'Freddy' Snell, recalled;

'"Freddy" immediately instructed all squadron aircraft to return to base. After landing, one of the pilots, Flg Off Tullet, was walking away from his aircraft when the groundcrew called him back. The leading-edge skin [of his Mosquito] had peeled back, leaving a gap. Our engineering officer, after looking at the aircraft, had the skin cut back to the main spar, where [a] gap between the main spar and scarf joint was revealed.'

That same day, as previously recounted, No 45 Sqn flight commander Sqn Ldr Don Edwards, with his navigator, Flg Off Eric Sandifer, were killed when HP921 broke up in the circuit on returning to Kumbhirgram. A clear pattern was emerging.

Almost immediately, all Mosquitos in non-operational units were grounded, whilst Nos 45 and 684 Sqns had to inspect their aircraft. World War 1 veteran aviator Sqn Ldr C J Chabot of the AIB flew in and worked with F G Myers, de Havilland's representative in-theatre, as well as the

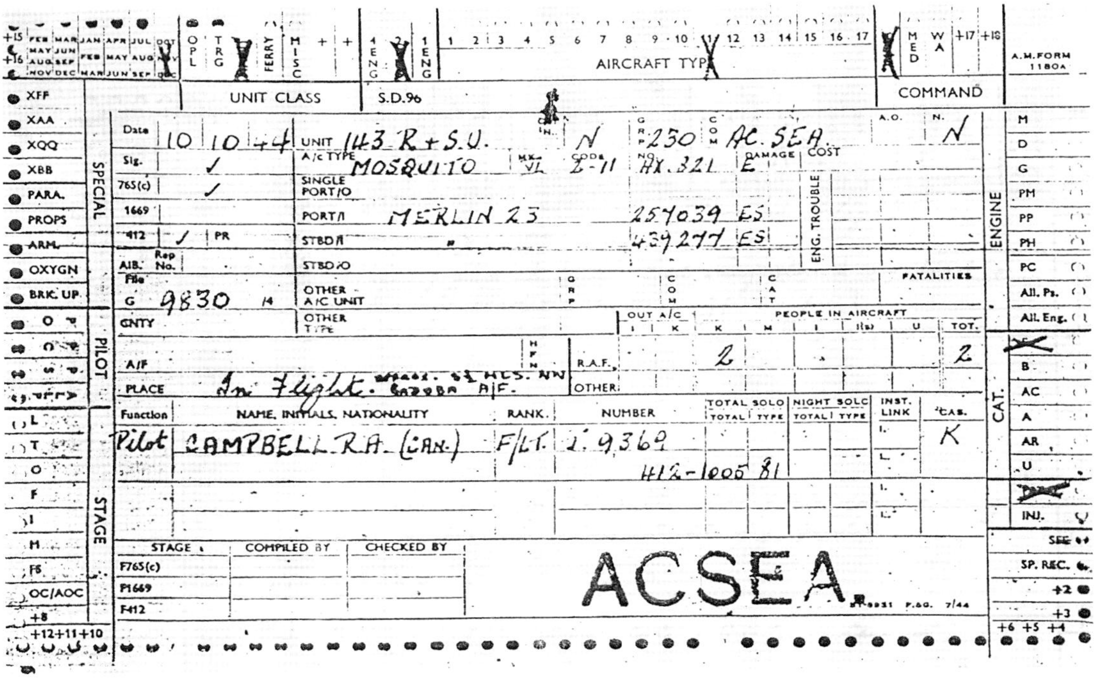

A.M. FORM 1180A

AIRCRAFT TYPE — UNIT CLASS — S.D.96 — COMMAND

Date: 10 10 44 — UNIT: 143 R + S.U. — N — 250 — AC. SEA. — N

A/C TYPE: MOSQUITO — Mk. VI — Z-11 — No. HX.821 — DAMAGE: E

PORT/I: MERLIN 23 — 257039 ES

STBD/I: 439277 ES

File G: 9830 14

PEOPLE IN AIRCRAFT: K 2 — TOT. 2

PLACE: In flight. ... NW ... A/F.

Function: Pilot — NAME, INITIALS, NATIONALITY: CAMPBELL R.A. (CAN.) — RANK: F/LT. — NUMBER: J.9369 — 412-1005 81 — CAS.: K

INJ.: K

ACSEA.

This Form 1180 records the loss of HX821. Flt Sgt Alf Pridmore, Flt Lt Campbell's navigator, should have been on the flight, as he explained. 'Dick was asked to test a "Mossie" whose exhaust shrouds had been burnt out, leaving no shield to the exhaust flames. Dick did not want to fly the aircraft, anticipating a fire risk, but the engineering officer wanted to go up in a "Mossie" and persuaded him it was safe, and to let him go in my place. I was watching from the ground and saw the wing break off at about 8000 ft and spin into the wild scrub away from the airfield.' Even though it notes that two people were killed, Flt Lt Rimell is not listed by name on the form (*Geoff Pridmore Collection*)

squadrons' engineers. Initial concerns focused on the scarf joint in the wing main spar. Chabot and Myers reported quickly;

'It cannot be definitively stated that these [crashes] are due to faulty manufacture or glue deterioration, but the onus appears to show that there are errors in the shaping of the wood making up the spar assembly. A common fault is that pieces of wood are so shaped that when assembled, essential elements do not make surface contact and no adhesion takes place. Under stress, the cover skin becomes detached and the modified box section wing assembly collapses. Until a reliable means of inspection and repair can be devised, all Mosquito Mk VIs at OTUs will be placed unserviceable.'

The Mosquitos' issues were serious enough to involve Geoffrey de Havilland, who joined Myers and Chabot when they visited the various squadrons equipped with the aircraft in India. Whilst with No 82 Sqn at Ranchi, de Havilland collected the wing from Flg Off Parker's ill-fated aircraft and sent it back to England. Flg Off Wambeek watched de Havilland inspecting Mosquitos;

'He knew exactly where to look for the trouble. With a fretsaw, he cut inspection panels in the wings of the squadron's remaining 17 aircraft and condemned 14 of them. Like everything else in wartime, skilled labour was in short supply, and the shadow factories constructing Mosquito wings had to make do with relatively unskilled carpenters. Where the scarf joints were imperfectly fashioned, the centre sections and outer sections had been set up in jigs and the gaps filled in with glue. The glue filling crumbled with extremes of temperature.

'Over dinner that evening, de Havilland told us that the next nine months' supply of Mosquito wings had already been stockpiled in the UK, and that there was little that could be done apart from rejecting those with badly flawed main spars. The invasion of Europe was in full swing, and every possible aircraft was required. This news did nothing to boost morale. Nor did it improve when later it was decided that four of the condemned aircraft could be put back into service after modifications [Mod. 638] had been carried out to strengthen the wings. All existing aircraft were also to have the same modifications carried out retrospectively.'

On 11 November, at Kumbhirgram, Geoffrey de Havilland led a further round of airframe inspections, focusing on HR-serialled aircraft newly arrived from Britain. At least 14 of No 45 Sqn's aeroplanes were found to be defective, with six being condemned. The next day, No 684 Sqn at Dum Dum, operating Mosquito FB VIs and PR XVIs, noted, 'Section of wingtip splicing on some aircraft found to be defective due to inferior workmanship at the factories building the components'.

An inadequate factor of safety, high-g manoeuvres, high control column loads, heat, humidity, casein glue and poor workmanship created a perfect storm for the Mosquito. The next day, all aircraft in OTUs in India were grounded until further notice. Squadron engineers visited Kanchrapara to learn how to complete detailed inspections of the mainplanes, which resulted in more FB VIs being classified as unserviceable upon their return. Like many aircrew, Flg Off Wambeek was concerned;

'In three months of training, we had lost three, and almost a fourth, aircraft due to structural failure – and of the remainder, ten were not repairable and dismantled for spares. To press home attacks against the enemy it is necessary to fly to the very limits of structural strength of one's aircraft. Squadron morale went to rock bottom.'

Mosquitos which could be rectified were flown to Kanchrapara, as Plt Off Bob Willis of No 47 Sqn, explained;

'On 15 November, following the grounding of all of our aircraft, I flew Mosquito HX943 to Kanchrapara. The flight was at a pre-determined speed, with instructions to make no violent manoeuvres and just deliver the aircraft safely. Provided the Mosquito arrived in one piece, it could be repaired and modified.'

The risk to aircrew in making such transit flights was never discussed.

On 20 November 1944, a report from another meeting by the AIB was issued. There had been a further 15 suspected airframe failures in Britain between July and September, but the committee had not investigated any failures abroad. Although the problems being experienced by the Mosquitos in India were clearly very serious, the aircraft were needed to force the Japanese retreat.

Four days later, Maj Hereward de Havilland (Geoffrey's brother, and managing director of de Havilland Australia) arrived in India on his way to Britain. On 26 November, he headed up a conference in Comilla that discussed the findings of the airframe investigation. No 45 Sqn's CO, Wg Cdr 'Johnny' Walker, and OC Wing HQ, Gp Capt E A Whiteley, were key participants in the conference, which concluded that the Mosquito did indeed have a future in India. Contradicting the earlier assessments, de Havilland reported that the failures were not caused by deterioration of glue, but by extensive shrinkage of airframes during the monsoon season. Many Mosquitos could, therefore, be repaired and returned to operations, supplemented by replacements ferried out from Britain. Rectified and replacement Mosquitos would first be supplied to Nos 45 and 82 Sqns, followed by Nos 47 and 110 Sqns in due course.

SHRINKAGE?

On 1 January 1945, during a meeting at the Ministry of Aircraft Production in London, Maj de Havilland presented a report on the Mosquitos' airframe failures in India, stating that 'the accidents were not caused by the deterioration of the glue but by shrinkage of the airframe during the wet monsoon season'. The Ministry accepted these findings, which was probably political expedience to prevent a loss in confidence by Mosquito crews. It also avoided handing the enemy a propaganda victory with the withdrawal of the aircraft from the theatre.

This conclusion was at odds with the more detailed investigation completed by Geoffrey de Havilland, Chabot and Myers, which identified clear evidence of manufacturing defects as noted in this extract from a report created by the AIB;

'This investigation was later confirmed by a team from the Ministry of Aircraft Production, which found faults in six Mosquito marks built at the Hatfield and Leavesden plants. The defects were similar, and none of the aircraft had been exposed to monsoon conditions or termite attack.'

The squadrons in India were not aware of the 1 January meeting, or its conclusions. They were just focused on receiving as many operational Mosquitos as possible.

On 2 January, Nos 45 and 82 Sqns received a signal calling for an inspection of the joints around the Mosquito's dinghy stowage hatch. Five of No 45 Sqn's aircraft were found to be faulty. Airframe fitter Aircraftman Cyril Norridge recalled. 'It was possible to pull off literally yards of ply, and the disintegrated glue would fly up in clouds, almost like French chalk.' The problem aircraft were immediately ferried to Kanchrapara for rectification, leaving the squadron short until replacements were delivered. At that time, No 82 Sqn had only four Mosquitos for operations, so the units pooled resources and worked together.

Another report, entitled 'Mosquito Structural Failures', was issued by the AIB on 24 February 1945. It stated that, 'During the period under review (October–December 1944) only four cases of structural failure were reported, all of which were investigated by this Branch.' None of the many failures in India were mentioned or reviewed. The committee was satisfied that failure rates were dropping. 'The rate for the quarter under review is 1 in 22,000 flying hours, which is a marked improvement on any previous rate. It indicates the modifications and other preventative actions are having beneficial results.'

The Mosquitos in India were never grounded again, although airframes still failed. Engineers continued to find ways to mitigate the issues, including painting the aircraft with silver dope and retiring Mosquitos used in the theatre after just 250 flying hours.

CHAPTER SIX

STRIKE FORCE

FB VI HR402/OB-C of No 45 Sqn provides the backdrop for RAAF and RNZAF aircrew gathered at Kumbhirgram on 7 January 1945. They are, from left to right, Flt Lt Jack Nankervis, Flg Offs Max Neill, Ernie Hallett, Bob Barclay (leaning against the propeller) and Rex Garnham (in the slouch hat), Flt Lt Arthur Huon and, facing them, squadron adjutant Flg Off Merv Nicholls (*State Library of Victoria*)

From early November 1944, No 45 Sqn's operations were restricted by the number of airworthy Mosquitos it possessed, averaging only four a day for the first week. On the 9th, the unit was tasked with mounting a seven-aircraft dawn raid on Meiktila airfield, the operation being led by Flt Lt 'Jock' Torrance. Each Mosquito was armed with four 500-lb 11-second delay bombs and had 'full ammo cans'.

The group planned to rendezvous at Mount Popa at 0620 hrs, and although Torrance was there at the appointed time, the others failed to meet up with him due to poor weather and effective enemy radio jamming. One Mosquito went for its secondary target and the others, arriving late, made their attacks separately.

Plt Off Emeny and Flt Sgt Yanota were flying their usual aircraft, HR374. Flg Off H M 'Nick' Nicholls RAAF and Flg Off Bob Barclay RAAF (navigator) flew as their wingmen. It was Yanota's 17th operation, and they routed to Pakokku, expecting to meet the others. He recalled;

'Visibility was down to zero because of a storm, so we returned to the river. Joining two other Mosquitos there, we journeyed south around the storm and Mount Popa and set course for Meiktila.'

As they crossed Meiktila Lake at low level, heavy AA fire opened up on them, hitting one of Emeny's engines. Then two 'Oscars' from 64th Sentai 'bounced the lame Mossie', repeatedly attacking. 'Bullets passed between me and the armour plate protecting Cliff's seat,' Yanota explained. 'Some bullets struck his armour plating, sending fragments into my face, and bullets struck the instrument panel. "Nick" Nicholls attacked one of the "Oscars" with his Mossie, but the other one performed a snap loop and got onto our tail. We hit 18 lbs boost and easily left the enemy aircraft behind'.

Nevertheless, HR374 seemed doomed, and Emeny radioed, 'We've had it.' Yanota continued, 'As our port engine was on fire, we had no choice but to crash land. After we hit the ground, the Mosquito soon stopped sliding, and I exited the aircraft, which was now in flames.' Emeny had been momentarily knocked out in the crash, and he suffered burns to his shoulders when the aircraft caught fire. He had also hurt his wrist and legs, and he needed Yanota – who was uninjured – to help him evacuate the wrecked Mosquito. Escaping from the scene, they were captured a few hours later by 'Burmese men armed with two spears and a Thompson machine gun'. Handed over to the IJA, they became PoWs.

The following day, No 45 Sqn's Mosquitos were grounded once again, and all but eight crews were given four days of leave. This time every Mosquito was inspected, even the newest, after which six were condemned and others sent for rectification. By 20 November it was clear that it would take some weeks before the unit would be fully operational again, so Wg Cdr Walker received orders from 3rd Tactical Air Force to detach most of his pilots to the communication squadrons of Nos 221 and 224 Groups, where they would fly Sentinel I/IIs and Tiger Moths in the forward operating areas whilst the Mosquitos were being repaired.

During the 'grounding', limited operations continued primarily against railway bridges, with Mosquitos sometimes being immediately refuelled and re-armed for a new crew.

On 12 December, the focus of No 45 Sqn's tasking changed to include IJAAF fighter airfields, with two aircraft dive-bombing Meiktila at dawn. Later that day, navigator Flt Sgt Alf Pridmore joined the squadron. Although trained on Mosquitos, he would have to develop his low-level navigating skills 'on the job', since he had previously specialised in

The thatched administration buildings at Kumbhirgram in late 1944 *(Second World War Experience Centre [SWWEC] – LEEWW.2001.1762 White, G W)*

high-level photo-reconnaissance. Pridmore's previous pilot, Flt Lt Dick Campbell RCAF, had been killed when Mosquito FB VI HX821 suffered an airframe failure during an air test over Bishnapur on 10 October 1944.

Serviceable aircraft had increased in number by 13 December, with nine operational Mosquitos available for No 45 Sqn. Five sorties were flown that day against Meiktila airfield and two against bridges. On the 14th, three aircraft targeted the same bridges, with two more being sent to attack an IJA transit camp at Monywa. Since the bridges were still usable, on 15 December six aircraft again bombed them, led by Wg Cdr Walker. This time they attacked from a range of heights down to 200 ft, using 11-second delays on the bombs. Again, they were unsuccessful – 'the only claim to the day's work was possible slight damage to one bridge'. Girder bridges, often with 'bypass' bridges nearby, were particularly challenging to destroy.

On the 16th, the pilots that had been detached to communication squadrons returned, whilst their squadronmates attempted to destroy IJA positions in the village of Gada. The next day, No 45 Sqn was tasked with attacking the IJA camp at Ye-U. Four Mosquitos targeted the camp in the morning, followed by a further four in the afternoon. Each dropped their bombs and then strafed it, hitting trucks and locos. Unfortunately, Plt Off Max Levey RAAF experienced engine trouble and was forced to feather his Mosquito's starboard engine. His navigator, Plt Off Harry Cargill RAAF, gave Levey a heading to divert to Yazagyo airstrip, where he managed to land but then crashed after losing control of the Mosquito. The aircraft caught fire once it came to halt, with the crew trapped in the wreckage. Both Levey and Cargill perished in the blaze that engulfed the Mosquito.

Even though it was still short of aircraft, No 82 Sqn was declared operational in mid-December. Most aircrew, along with a small number of Mosquitos, duly transferred to Kumbhirgram, where they awaited their groundcrew. Once settled in, squadron CO Wg Cdr Lionel 'Bill' Hudson was keen to fly his unit's first Mosquito operation. 'My flight into Burma from Assam that day [19 December] was my own bright idea,' he recalled. 'It was a journey that was not really necessary.'

With fellow Australian Flt Lt Dick 'Scotty' McKenzie as his wingman, Hudson led the two Mosquitos aloft at 1030 hrs. Having passed through the gap between the Naga and Chin Hills, they quickly descended and flattened out just above the treetops for a low-level 'rhubarb', seeking targets of opportunity. Hudson continued;

'Before us was the Irrawaddy River, broad and smooth and lightly veiled in the morning mist. It beckoned. I swished down and skimmed it. Then there was a jolting crash, a jarring note and a freezing of the music inside my stomach.'

Hudson had touched the water and bent the tips of his port propeller. The Mosquito was unflyable and, before long, he and his navigator crashed into the jungle in Japanese-held territory near the Chindwin and Irrawaddy rivers' confluence. With their legs lacerated, as they struggled away from the remains of their aircraft their enemies were already approaching. At first, the Japanese troops just stood and stared, but a Sikh soldier with them knelt and aimed his rifle at the downed aviators. Hudson and Flt Sgt Jack Shortis were PoWs. McKenzie reported that he had last seen the CO's aircraft 15 miles east southeast of Pakokku.

RAAF pilot Flg Off Bill Taylor of No 45 Sqn flew 44 Mosquito intruder sorties over Burma, and 65 operations in total (*Sue Cox Collection*)

With Hudson posted as 'Missing', Sqn Ldr 'Freddy' Snell, No 82 Sqn's senior flight commander, was made CO of the unit. In due course, he was promoted to wing commander.

Both Nos 45 and 82 Sqn flew operations on Christmas Day, with the latter despatching two aircraft in the morning that were then back in time for their crews to enjoy a traditional Christmas lunch. Later, No 45 Sqn flew six night sorties, with aircraft departing between 1826–2024 hrs. Meanwhile, Nos 47 and 110 Sqn were still waiting to receive Mosquitos at Ranchi and Yelahanka, respectively.

On 26 December, four No 45 Sqn Mosquitos were tasked with bombing the IJAAF airfield at Heho. One of these aircraft (HR447), loaded with extra fuel in wing tanks and armed with 500-lb bombs fitted with 11-second delay fuses, took off at 1604 hrs with Flg Off Bill Taylor RAAF at the controls and WO Ken Putnam as his navigator. After bombing Heho, the Mosquitos formed up to strafe the airfield, as Taylor explained;

'I was No 3 in [a] line abreast [formation], and we came in at full speed of about 350 mph at zero feet. The Japs hit us with everything they had. One gunner got me in his sights and I could see his tracers flying over my starboard wing. I couldn't go up, as I would fly into his bullets, or go down, as we were at zero feet, so I just had to keep going.'

HR447 was hit in the starboard engine, emitting a stream of black smoke. With the propeller feathered and fire extinguished, they managed to escape. Unable to cross a mountain between Heho and home, Taylor and Putnam headed for Kalemyo, which, they had been told, had night landing facilities. 'In fact, it was the only Allied landing strip in Burma at the time', Taylor recalled. 'Eventually, we located the strip and circled, firing off the colours of the period, which changed every six hours. Then we sent off a red one to indicate distress. They signalled back an instruction to wait.

'After a while I could see something like cars moving up from the base to the aerodrome, and I said to Ken, "These buggers haven't got any lights!" They were moving trucks up to shine on the strip. They parked three trucks diagonally on either side of the strip where we would make our approach, leaving their lights on to indicate where the ground was. They then flashed a green light for us to go in.'

Knowing that it was a short strip for Hurricanes, Taylor approached it slightly faster to ensure better control once on the ground;

'I knew I would have trouble pulling up. Also, I didn't know whether we had a puncture in the starboard landing gear, so I told Ken to keep his hand on the undercarriage handle and be ready to pull the wheels up on landing if I felt any movement to the right. Luckily, all went well, and I stopped right on the end of the strip.' (*Text continues on page 57*)

COLOUR PLATES

1
Mosquito F II DZ695 of No 27 Sqn, RAF Agartala, India, 11 April 1943

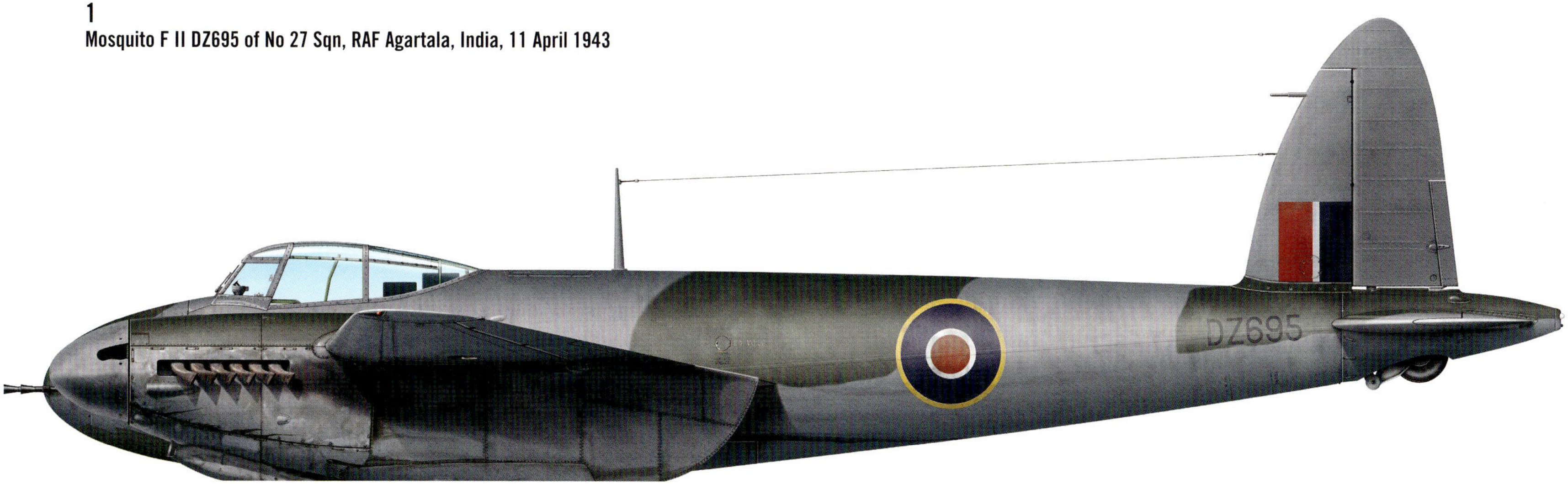

2
Mosquito FB VI HJ811 of No 27 Sqn, RAF Allahabad, India, October 1943

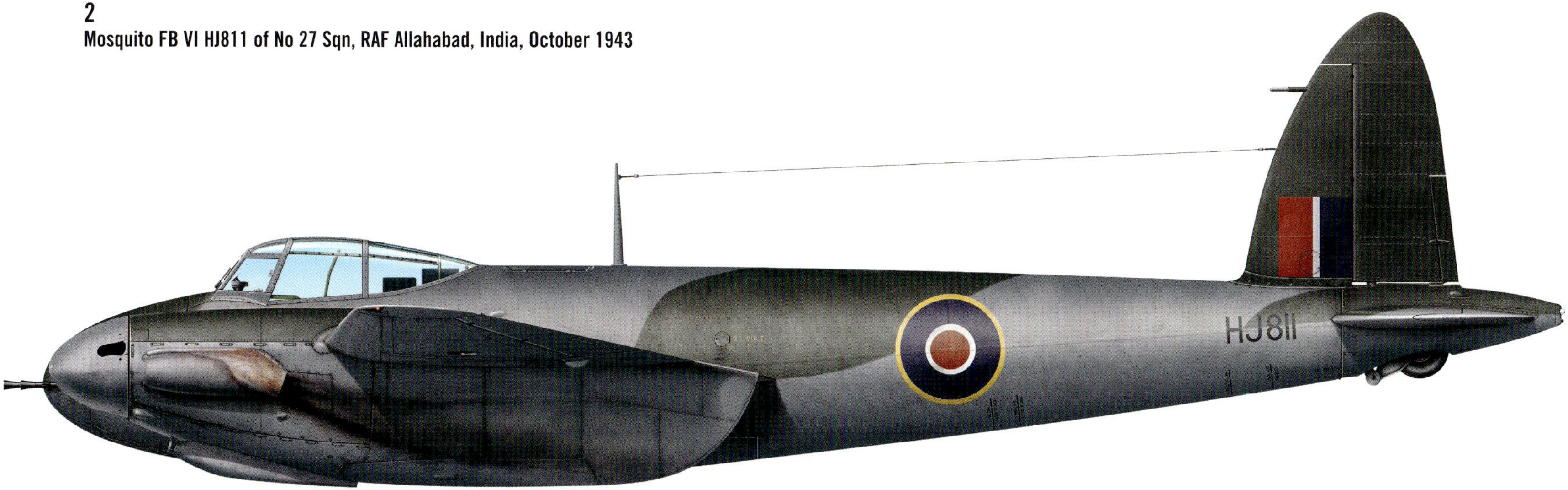

3

Mosquito FB VI HX821/K of No 27 Sqn, RAF Agartala, India, February 1944

4

Mosquito PR IX LR445/F of No 684 Sqn, RAF Dum Dum, India, April 1944

5
Mosquito FB VI HP939/OB-A of No 45 Sqn, RAF Amarda Road, India, May 1944

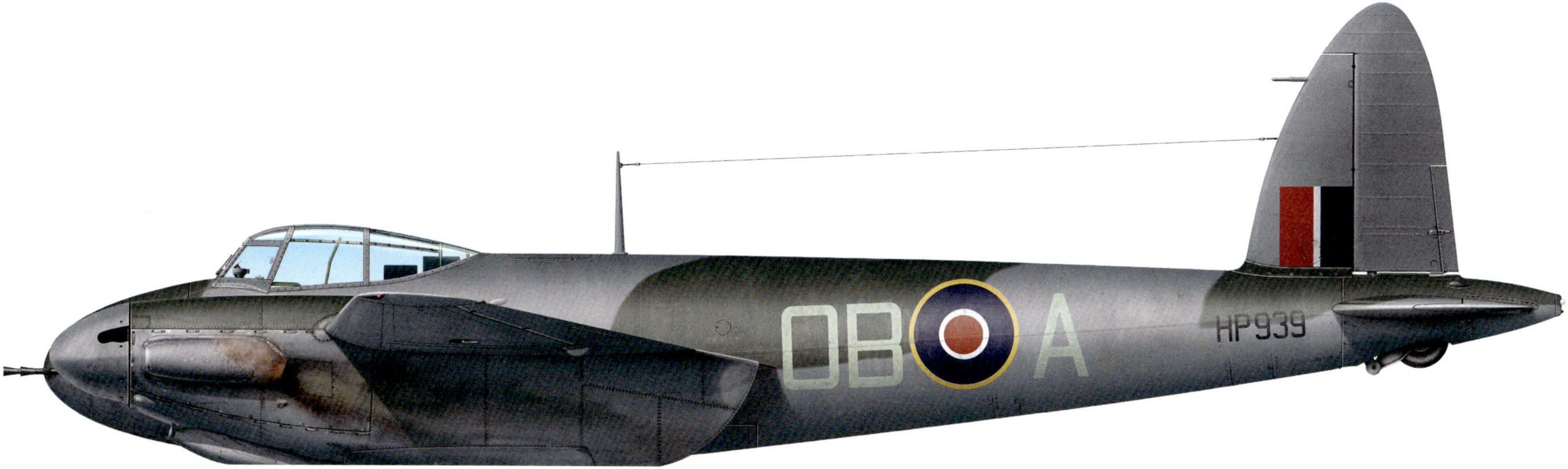

6
Mosquito FB VI HP867/OB-Z of No 45 Sqn, RAF Dalbumgarh, India, 24 June 1944

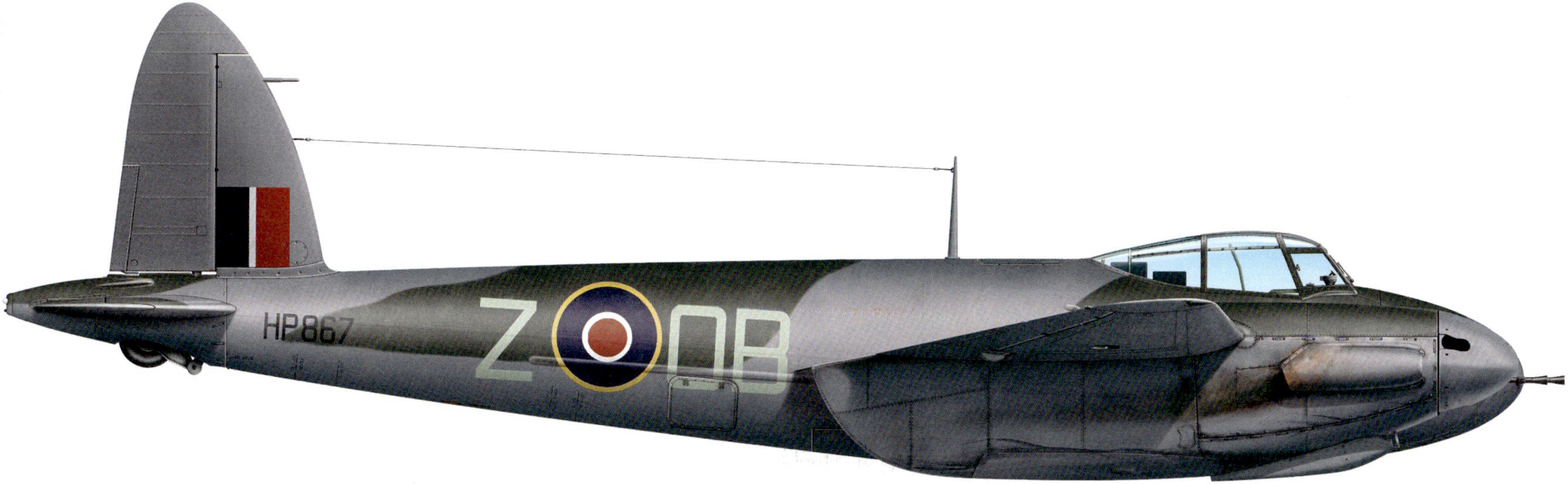

7

Mosquito FB VI HP886/UX-H of No 82 Sqn, RAF Kolar, India, 13 September 1944

8

Mosquito PR XVI NS688 (subsequently assigned to No 684 Sqn), RAF Dum Dum, India, November 1944

9
Mosquito FB VI HR374/OB-Z of No 45 Sqn, RAF Kumbhirgram, India, 9 November 1944

10
Mosquito PR XVI NS645/P of No 684 Sqn, RAF Alipore, India, late 1944

11

Mosquito FB VI HR403/UX-B of No 82 Sqn, RAF Kumbhirgram, India, 19 December 1944

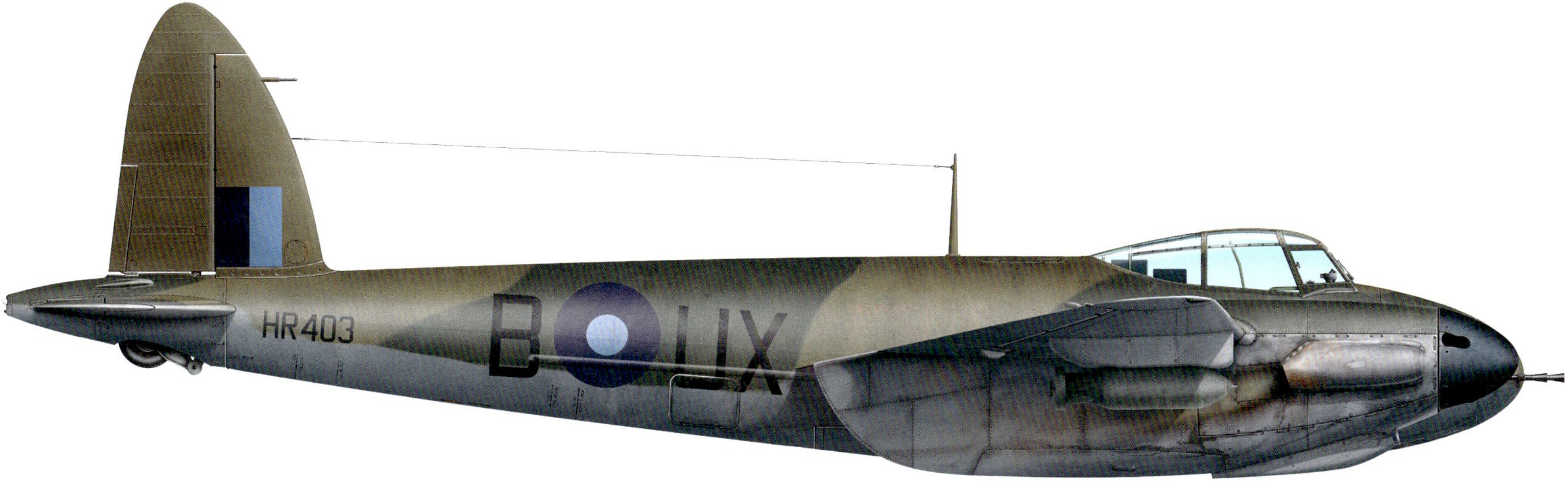

12

Mosquito FB VI HR402/OB-C of No 45 Sqn, RAF Kumbhirgram, India, 7 January 1945

13
Mosquito FB VI HR567/OB-D of No 45 Sqn, RAF Kumbhirgram, India, 10 February 1945

14
Mosquito FB VI HR567/OB-F of No 45 Sqn, RAF Kumbhirgram, India, 4 April 1945

15
Mosquito FB VI RF700/KU-V of No 47 Sqn, RAF Kinmagan, Burma, 30 April 1945

16
Mosquito FB VI RF582/VE-K of No 110 Sqn, RAF Joari, India, 2 May 1945

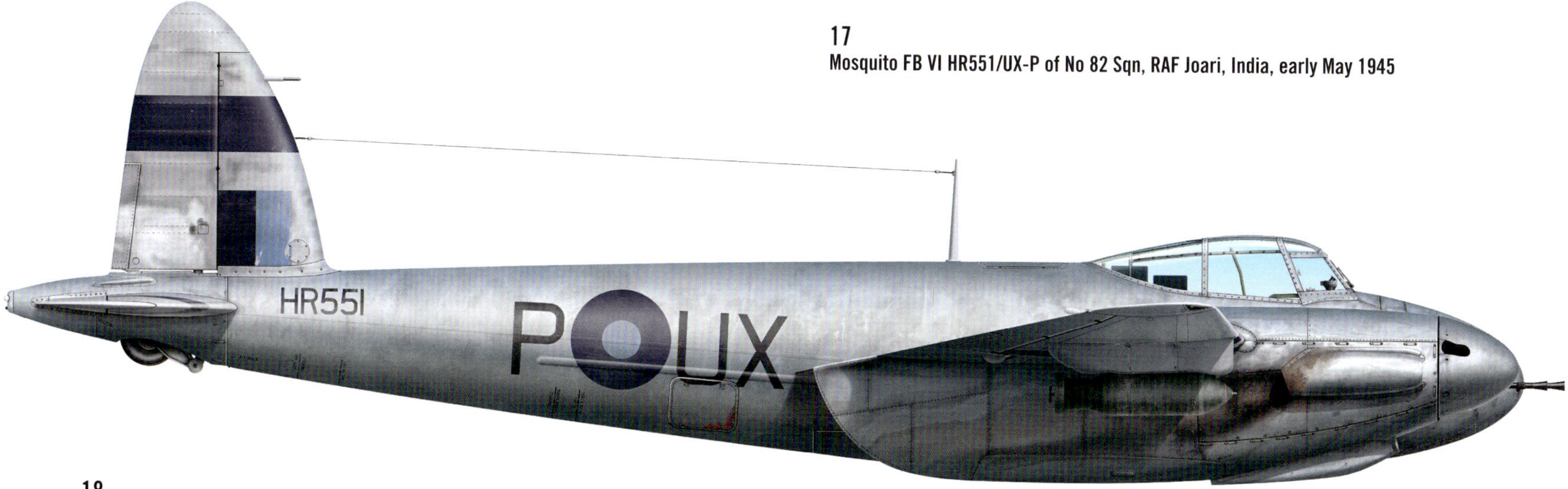

17
Mosquito FB VI HR551/UX-P of No 82 Sqn, RAF Joari, India, early May 1945

18
Mosquito PR 34 RG203/E of No 684 Sqn, Cocos Island, July 1945

19

Mosquito FB VI RF711/A of No 211 Sqn, RAF Yelahanka, India, early July 1945

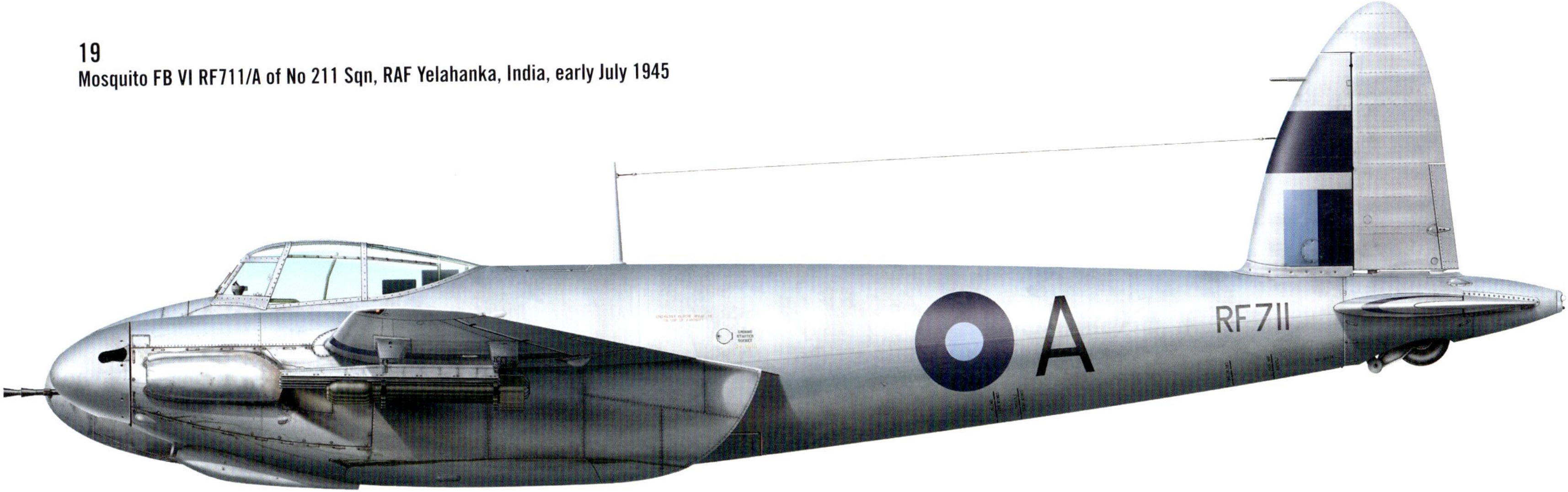

20

Mosquito PR XVI MM367/U of No 684 Sqn, RAF Alipore, India, July 1945

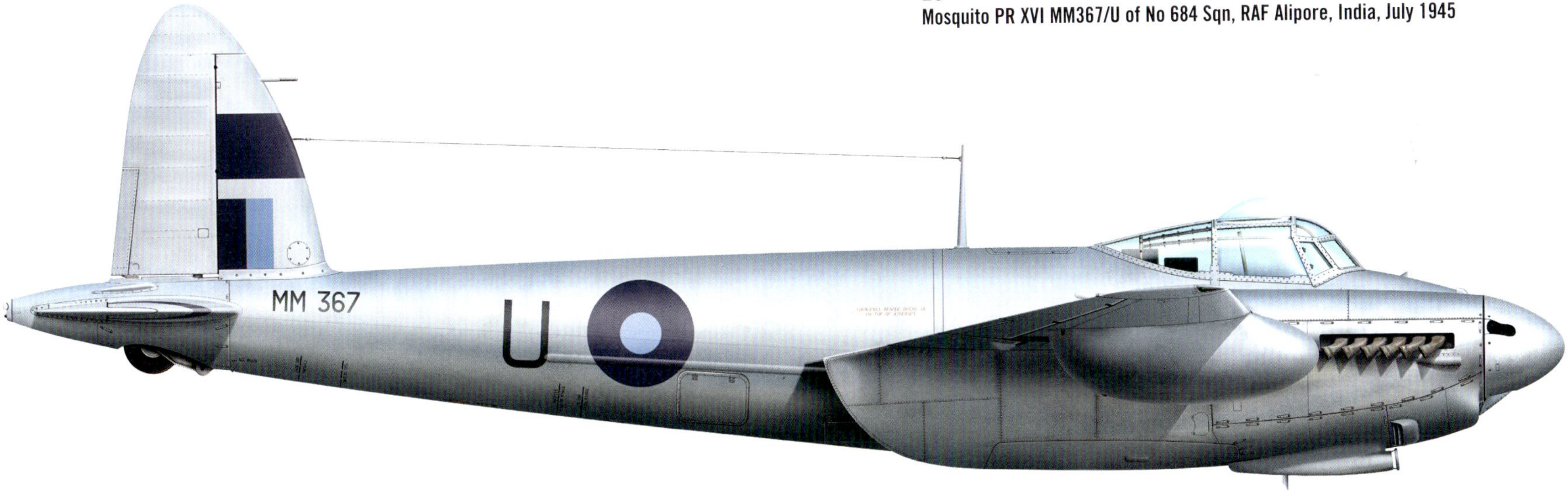

21
Mosquito FB VI HR562/VE-T of No 110 Sqn, RAF Hmawbi, Burma, 20 August 1945

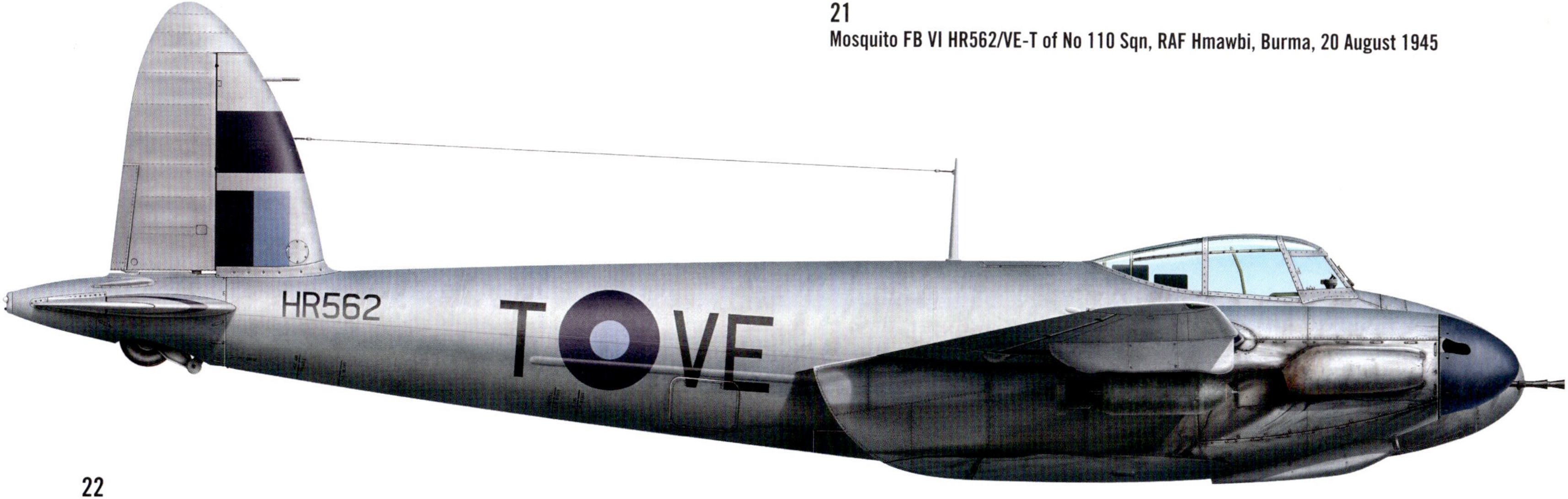

22
Mosquito FB 40 A52-500/NA-A of No 1 Sqn RAAF, Labuan Island, August 1945

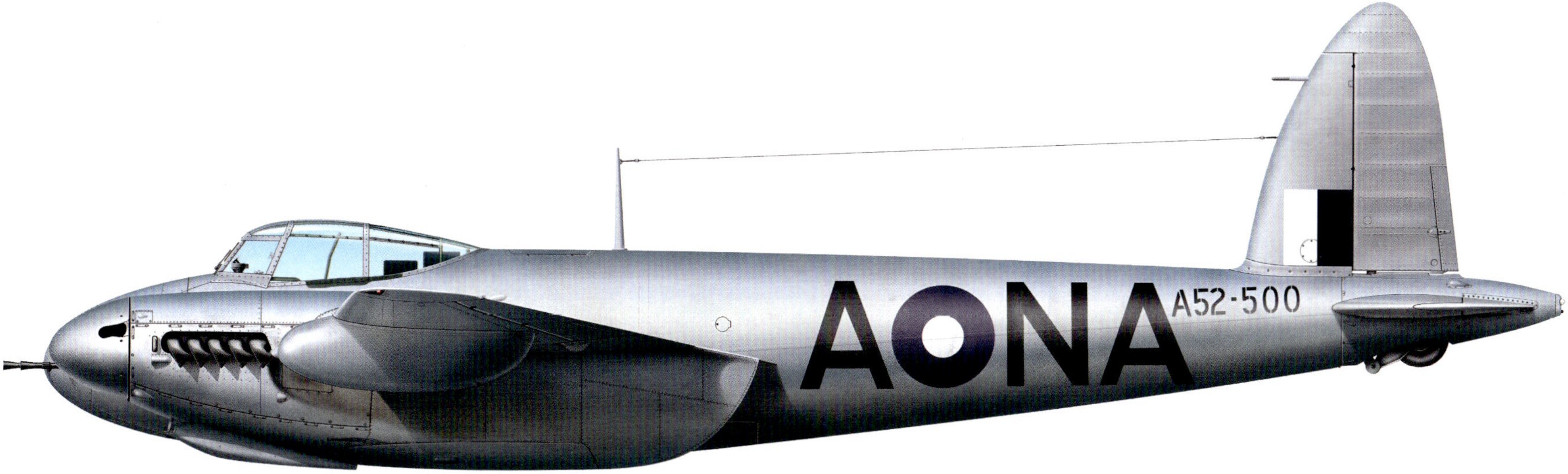

They were greeted by an irate wing commander who told them that the facility was not supposed to be operational until the following night. The pre-flight briefing given to the No 45 Sqn crews had been 24 hours premature. However, for Taylor and Putnam it was a life saver. 'We would never have made it back without Kalemyo. I received a "Green Endorsement" on my logbook for exceptional flying ability.'

Sadly, that same day, Flg Offs Ken Dorricott and Hank Wilson of No 82 Sqn were not so lucky. They were posted as 'Missing, believed killed' when they failed to return from their sortie, HR394 having crashed near Daungtaung.

With the waxing moon after Christmas, in addition to flying daytime sorties, No 82 Sqn aircrews also needed to be 'signed off' for night ops. Each day, once darkness fell, four or five crews flew circuits one night, local area flying the next and, finally, completed night sector reconnaissance.

On 29 December, six No 45 Sqn Mosquitos led by Sqn Ldr Torrance were tasked with another dawn dive-bombing raid on two airfields. Walsh and Orsborn flew HR456 on the operation, the former recalling;

'On a few occasions we would rendezvous with other Mosquitos (usually about six of them) at the target, climb to 10,000 ft and then, one by one, we would dive-bomb and strafe the target, with each aeroplane peeling off as they completed the raid.'

Four of the six targeted Meiktila and two would attack nearby Thedaw airfield. Flying independently in the dark over Japanese-held territory, they rendezvoused just before dawn over the Irrawaddy, north of Meiktila. Having climbed to height over their targets, each aircraft dive-bombed in turn from 12,000 ft down to 3000 ft. When the others had completed their attacks, Walsh closed the throttles, opened the radiator shutters and rolled his Mosquito into a steep dive towards Meiktila airfield, with Orsborn calling out each 1000-ft decrease.

Although the others had experienced meagre AA fire, as Walsh positioned his aircraft to release his bombs 'the Japs put up a considerable amount of heavy flak'. After releasing his bombs, Walsh started pulling through 'the squash', powering up the Merlins during levelling off and then banking to return at low-level to strafe the airfield.

Having been the last to attack, as they climbed away to regroup, Walsh asked Orsborn to count the aircraft he could see in order to check that everyone was alright. Scanning the dawn skies around them, he counted 'One, two, three, four, five, six, seven, eight'. 'What?', exclaimed Walsh. 'We have gained two!' Two 'Oscars' had joined No 45 Sqn's Mosquitos, and Walsh saw that one was lining up to attack Torrance's aircraft. He called a warning to his flight commander and slammed his throttles fully open, hauling his Mosquito onto the tail of the 'Oscar' already firing tracer at Torrance's port wing. Walsh fired from about 200 yards. 'I managed to get a prolonged cannon and machine gun burst at one and I believe I damaged it.'

The Mosquitos had been bounced by six 'Oscars' and a Ki-44 'Tojo' from the northwest, but only the two Ki-43s came close enough to pose any real threat. After Walsh's successful counterattack, the IJAAF pilots lost their enthusiasm and kept their distance. The six Mosquito crews sought the relative protection of low-level, completing their hour-long journey over Japanese-held territory towards the Naga and Lushai Hills.

Sorties continued through to the end of the month when, on 31 December, Nos 45 and 82 Sqns were tasked with their first combined bombing operation on Thedaw airfield. As noted in No 82 Sqn's Operations Record Book (ORB), 'Much excitement today – our first bombing operation'.

Four aircraft from each unit attacked in line abreast right across the runway, running roughly north to south, together with dispersal areas and aircraft pens down both sides of the strip. All four of No 45 Sqn's Mosquitos and three from No 82 Sqn were armed with two 500-lb Mk IV bombs fitted with 11-second delay fuses. The fourth No 82 Sqn aircraft strafed 'anything that presented itself on the airfield as a suitable target for his guns'. Some aircraft got ahead of others, causing potential danger from falling bombs. Even so, 'As everyone cheerfully remarked, it was a start'.

JANUARY 1945

Following the dinghy stowage areas issue, on 3 January No 45 Sqn could only field 14 aircraft and No 82 Sqn four for Operations *Nasty I* and *Nasty II* against two large communication centres at Maymyo and Thazi aimed at forcing the IJA to use radios, not telephones. Armed with two 500-lb bombs each, the aircraft were despatched through the day in four waves starting at 0816 hrs for Thazi, then 0829 hrs for Maymyo, 1335 hrs for Thazi and 1400 hrs for Maymyo. Unfortunately, in the first wave, HR515 suffered engine problems just after take-off and ploughed into the jungle about five miles from the airfield. WO John McQueen RNZAF and navigator WO Bill Edwards were killed. However, both communication centres were substantially destroyed.

A 'chota' monsoon over the next few days made it impossible to fly across the hills to Burma. Then, on 8 January, in 'perfect' weather, 15 No 45 Sqn aircraft and five from No 82 Sqn set off in waves to attack the waterfront at Sagaing and 'rhubarb' the Irrawaddy as far as Chauk. The sorties were successful, with relatively little opposition.

Newly arrived No 45 Sqn Mosquito FB VI HR526 showing the word *SNAKE* introduced in May 1943 to prevent aircraft intended for India being 'hi-jacked' during transit to another theatre. The aircraft is seen here at Kumbhirgram shortly before it was damaged by AA fire during an attack on Paleik and subsequently suffered an undercarriage collapse on landing on 9 January 1945. The Mosquito was repaired shortly thereafter (*SWWEC – LEEWW.2001.1762 White, G W*)

The following day, in 'grim' weather, No 45 Sqn launched ten Mosquitos against a target at Paleik, followed by a 'rhubarb' towards Chauk. Three of the first wave made it to the target despite the conditions, bombing from altitudes of 50–80 ft. Opposition was accurate, with HR526, flown by Flg Offs Freddie Fortune and Joe Mears, suffering hits to its undercarriage, a wheel and port inner fuel tank. At 1313 hrs, when Fortune touched down at Kumbhirgram, the undercarriage collapsed. Luckily, the damage inflicted was pretty light, and within a few weeks HR526 was back on the flightline. Later, at 1630 hrs, Flg Off Bob Wilson RCAF and WO Bill Hayward could not lower the undercarriage on HR455, so they were forced to carry out a belly landing on the kutcha strip. Both walked away.

On 12 January, four No 45 Sqn aircraft were tasked with a dawn bombing raid on Thedaw airfield. Departing at 0452 hrs, two minutes later, mission leader Flt Lt Huon, Wilson and Hayward suffered engine failure in HR492 as they took off. The Mosquito crashed into the jungle and erupted in flames just one-and-a-half miles from the runway, with both crewmen being killed. The remaining two aircraft took off over their crash site a few minutes later. The three Mosquitos attacked Thedaw from 0617 hrs. Frustratingly, one Mosquito's bombs would not release, so Huon brought them home after they had patrolled Thedaw for 30 minutes.

Later that morning, both Nos 45 and 82 Sqns each launched four pairs of Mosquitos 'to attack the Jap stronghold of Monywa'. The No 45 Sqn aircraft had dropped bombs on the target, with crews subsequently reporting that 'uncountable small 20/40 ft sampans were strafed by these aircraft and many strikes were seen'. Two pairs from No 82 Sqn took off at about 0950 hrs and dropped their bombs 'in close concentration south of the jail'. The first Mosquito pair then hit about 60 sampans during its strafing run, with the second pair striking a further 20. No 82 Sqn finished a busy day with a four-aircraft operation again targeting river traffic, damaging three camouflaged 50-ft motor launches on the Mytinge River.

That same afternoon, a flight of Ki-43 'Oscars', probably from Meiktila, attacked the recently recaptured forward operating strip at Onbauk, destroying two Dakotas on the ground and shooting down two more transports. SEAC reacted immediately to protect the Allied transports. From 14 January, they would establish a dawn-to-dusk patrol over Meiktila and Thedaw airfields. Both Nos 45 and 82 Sqns would be tasked with keeping the IJAAF aircraft on the ground during the morning, with No 45 Sqn bombing and then patrolling from dawn until 0800 hrs. Relieving them, No 82 Sqn would bomb Meiktila and Thedaw again, and patrol until Thunderbolts took over the tasking at 1100 hrs.

On 14 January, Walsh and Orsborn were one of eight No 45 Sqn crews tasked with attacking the airfields. They dive-bombed Thedaw from 9000 ft, releasing their four 500-lb bombs at 6000 ft, before patrolling both Meiktila and Thedaw at 4000–6000 ft for 50 minutes. Later, eight more crews from No 82 Sqn were tasked with undertaking the same mission, operating in four sections that each completed about an hour of patrolling after their initial dive-bombing attacks. Flg Off Wambeek reported that his bombs hit Thedaw's main runway about 600 yards from its southern end.

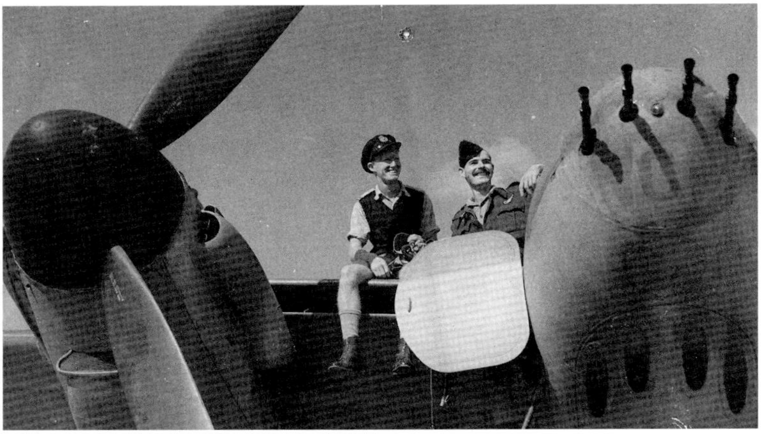

RAAF pilot Flg Off Peter Ewing and his navigator, WO Conrie 'Pinky' Pinkerton, pose on FB VI HR402/OB-C on 7 January 1945. They flew this aircraft on an operation to Meiktila on 14 January. The following day, HR402 was shot down by Ki-43s north of Thedaw, killing Flt Lt Ron Goodwin and Flg Off Samuel Potts (*Richard Ewing Collection*)

The next day, 'Bad luck again dogged the squadron [that] morning'. After an early briefing, three No 45 Sqn aircraft, piloted by Nicholls, Flt Lt Ron Goodwin and Walsh, took off at 0500 hrs so that they could be over Meiktila and Thedaw at dawn. Unfortunately, less than an hour into the sortie, Walsh was forced to jettison his bombs and return to base after the onset of technical problems. The two remaining aircraft continued to Meiktila, dive-bombing it at about 0630 hrs amidst heavy but inaccurate AA fire. Nicholls described what happened during the mission;

'We took off in company with Goodwin and [Flg Off Samuel] Potts, patrolling at "Angels 10" [10,000 ft] over the Jap airfields of Meiktila, Thedaw and Kagaung. The Japs obviously contacted the airfield at Heho, as we soon spotted four aircraft boring out of the sun and quickly warned the other crew. To our amazement, the other crew took no action, so we literally screamed over the R/T for them to "Break!"

'The first "Oscar" hit as Ron Goodwin was slowly turning to port and was acknowledging our warning over the R/T. These words were the last he ever spoke, as the remaining fighters bored in on him in succession and the Mossie went straight down and hit the ground in a tremendous explosion. There were no survivors. That left us facing four enemy aircraft, so we dived for the deck and hit 18 lbs boost and were doing 550 IAS [sic] and escaped.'

The downed Mosquito, HR402, crashed about eight miles north of Thedaw.

Nicolls radioed four pairs of approaching No 82 Sqn Mosquitos about the 'bandits'. Now aware that there were 'Oscars' in the area, Sqn Ldr Chris Gotch, leading the pair in HR406, decided to change their attack run on the target to low-level. At 0818 hrs, the Mosquitos swept east to west at deck-level over Meiktila at 300 mph. The aircraft of Flg Off Benison, following only seconds behind the lead Mosquito, was damaged by the bomb blast and one of the weapon's detonators. According to No 82 Sqn's ORB;

'The aircraft were just over the strip when A.A. opened up. It was intense, accurate and of all calibres – bursts of Bofors being observed all around the aircraft – as well as tracer from other 20 mm and other L.M.G. [light machine gun] posts. A 20 mm shell entered S/Ldr. Gotch's aircraft through the nose and, narrowly missing his left knee, passed through to the rear of the aircraft, filling the cockpit with smoke. S/Ldr. Gotch leaned forward to peer through the smoke and thereby had a narrow escape, for another 20 mm shell entered the cockpit, through the Perspex cockpit at his left, almost severing the wires of his Sutton harness, and bruised his shoulder. The shell struck F/Sgt. [Basil] Felsenstein in the face, smashing his face below the nose, and passed out through the Perspex blister on the starboard side.'

Although the aircraft had been hit by six 20-mm cannon shells in total, Gotch managed to break northeast towards safety and help for his mortally wounded navigator, Basil Felsenstein. Benison's aircraft was also hit many times over the strip, and he took avoiding action by flying over Meiktila Lake. It was an unfortunate decision, because he too was engaged by heavy and accurate AA fire, sometimes bursting on the lake and throwing columns of water up around his aircraft. Having run the gauntlet, he managed to catch up with HR406 about 20 miles to the north and escorted Gotch back to base, which, due to poor weather conditions, was the nearest available airfield.

Gotch's navigator remained conscious for much of the flight back to Kumbhirgram, lapsing into a coma shortly before he landed at 1000 hrs. Flt Sgt Felsenstein was rushed to Silchar Hospital, where he died two hours later.

A few minutes behind Gotch and Benison, the next No 82 Sqn pair attacked Thedaw at low-level and were also met by a hail of accurate AA fire. The ORB noted;

'On the way out, F/Sgt. Armstrong, in taking evasive action, hit a tree, inflicting severe damage on his aircraft, large sections of both leading edges being torn away and the port propeller and spinner badly battered.' Although damaged, the Mosquito was still flyable and Armstrong managed to return it to base. In the third wave, shortly before reaching the target, WO John McDonald's aircraft started leaking glycol in its starboard engine, so he had to feather it, then dropped his bombs 'fused' and headed for home. His section leader, Flt Lt McKenzie, scored a direct hit on the centre of the runway at Kagaung and damaged an 'Oscar' on the ground.

In the final wave, just before Plt Off Ted Thynne RAAF released his bombs over Meiktila, he felt a shock as his aircraft suffered damage to the port wing and canopy – a piece of stone was removed from his wing when he landed. All of No 82 Sqn's aircraft were accounted for when, after 200 miles of flying on one engine, McDonald completed a tricky landing at Talihal.

That evening, No 45 Sqn CO Wg Cdr Walker penned letters of condolence. To Flt Lt Ron Goodwin's parents, he wrote;

'The work that this squadron is doing is more dangerous than most, and we have not been without our losses. In fact our losses have been fairly heavy. This is a terrible war, but never so terrible as when it strikes so closely as this. I am proud to have known Ron. Men of his calibre and loyalty are indeed few and far between.'

Five No 45 Sqn aircraft were despatched to attack Meiktila again on 16 January, which was followed by a 24-hour unit stand-down. On the 18th, No 45 Sqn flew three waves of four aircraft to 'bomb and strafe' an IJA headquarters building at Kokko. Three aircraft in the first wave were damaged by hostile fire and debris. Amongst the Mosquitos hit was the CO's aircraft, and he was forced to feather an engine and make an emergency landing at Kalemyo. The remaining two returned to base. By late-afternoon, after the third wave, the target building in Kokko had been destroyed, with five fires raging. It was a successful day, with the intruders also strafing many sampans and launches.

Giving up waiting for its Mosquitos, No 47 Sqn arrived at Kumbhirgram with Beaufighter Xs and commenced operations on 20 January. Meanwhile, Nos 45 and 82 Sqns' operational load intensified.

During the morning of 26 January, No 45 Sqn despatched four Mosquitos, led by Sqn Ldr Torrance, to bomb a suspected petrol dump in the jail area of Fort Dufferin, at Mandalay. The crews planned for low-level release using bombs with 11-second delay fuses.

To maximise accuracy, recently promoted WO Walsh dived down to an altitude of just 600 ft before releasing the bombs. To his surprise, they exploded immediately just underneath the Mosquito and rocked it with the blast. The bombs were perfectly on target, resulting in a huge ball of fire from the exploding petrol dump which briefly engulfed the aircraft. As Walsh dryly recalled, 'At least, as we flew out of the inferno, we knew that the mission had been a success'. With Fort Dufferin in flames behind them, Walsh and Orsborn were relieved that their Mosquito had no signs of damage. Their attacks attracted some AA fire, but it was not very accurate.

Before returning to base, the four aircraft strafed opportunity targets along the Lashio road towards Nawngkhio, with Walsh shooting up three vehicles. After landing back at Kumbhirgram, he and Orsborn found the tailfin of one of their bombs embedded in the fuselage of their aircraft – another very close shave.

The aircrew were not happy with the 11-second delay fuses, the squadron ORB noting;

'Low-level bombing operations have had to be curtailed due to the doubtful functioning of the 11-second delay fuses. New ones have recently been received, and the squadron will carry out low-level sorties when the target necessitates it.'

WO Walsh of No 45 Sqn strafes sampans on the Chindwin River from very low-level in January 1945 (*Author's Collection*)

Operational tasking continually increased. Mosquitos from No 45 Sqn hit the oilfields at Yenangyaung, IJA installations in Mandalay, IJAAF airfields at Heho, Thedaw, Meiktila and Nawngkio, the Fourteenth Army bridgehead on the eastern banks of the Irrawaddy, bridges and railways, culminating with an attack on an IJA stronghold in the village of Ywabo. Meanwhile, No 82 Sqn attacked enemy positions in Mandalay, as well as Meiktila, Heho and Thedaw airfields, almost daily. It also targeted AA gun positions near Singu and the Fourteenth Army's Irrawaddy bridgehead, before completing a busy month of operations with an attack on a large concentration of IJA troops in the village of Tonbo.

Finally, there was good news for No 110 Sqn at Yelahanka. On 25 January, unit CO Wg Cdr Arthur 'Soapy' Saunders received the signal that his squadron had been awaiting. 'Signal 956, dated 24 January 1945, from B.A.F., S.E.A., orders the allotment of six Mosquito Aircraft from C.M.U. to 110 Squadron'. The aircraft were collected immediately to start the unit's Mosquito conversion.

Both Wg Cdrs Walker and Snell still had concerns about the Mosquito's structural weaknesses, since the modifications had not addressed the underlying problems. Walker was outspoken in his month-end report;

'Seeing that the squadron has been grounded three times since October with suspected structural weaknesses, it is amazing to find that no crews have any question about possible weaknesses today. It is therefore most alarming to hear that all Mosquitos are to be painted white as a final safety measure, which will reduce the internal heat in the wings. I should be impressed if any Mosquito designer can convince me and my crews that a white Mosquito is safe to fly and a camouflaged one is not. From an operational standpoint, the proposal is too stupid to warrant comment. To date this development has not been passed on to crews.'

FEBRUARY 1945

On 1 February, Flt Lt G F Mahoney and WO Roy Trew of No 82 Sqn were on a night raid on Heho airfield when they were hit by AA fire. Mahoney recalled;

'The weather had become very bad and we diverted to Kalemyo, but Kalemyo had been caught before [at night] by intruders and declined to put up a flarepath. We had now been airborne for six hours and could not wait for first light. With about ten minutes of fuel remaining, we headed a little way towards the Chindwin, feathered the starboard "prop" and abandoned [the aircraft]. I "discovered" a new experience by hitting the back of my neck on the tailplane as I left through the side exit.

'Eventually, I landed in habitation, and I immediately sought to know where my navigator was. I found it difficult to get this message across. There was a lot of beating of drums going on, and eventually the penny dropped that this was broadcast signalling, and distant replies could be heard. I believed I understood that Roy was safe some 20 miles down the Chindwin. We took a dugout and paddles, and lo and behold there he was, standing beside the Chindwin, expecting us! We were at Mawleik, on the Upper Chindwin, a remote supply-drop strip. They had a radio and it took days to get through to Kalemyo. The supply drop strip was made good enough to tempt an RAF Stinson Sentinel to fly in, and we were lifted out, one by one.'

Upon his return to No 82 Sqn, Mahoney was checked over by the unit's medical officer, Flt Lt Dawes, who reported that he seemed 'quite unaffected by what must be considered as one of the worst hazards of aerial warfare in this part of the world. In fact, he gave the impression that he had more confidence as a result of the incident'.

1 February saw No 45 Sqn start the month with a daylight attack on the 'oil village of Lanywa, on the Irrawaddy, where the Japs are believed to be constructing defence works'. They dive-bombed from 6000 ft down to 2000 ft, before 'rhubarbing' small vessels along the river, striking 'approximately 100 20/30 ft sampans'. That night, No 82 Sqn bombed Lanywa, after which the unit visited it daily through to the 4th, degrading its facilities.

Mosquitos from No 45 Sqn, meanwhile, completed nocturnal bombing raids on Myitnge bridge. On the night of 4 February, they visited the IJAAF airfield at Annisakan, hitting it with glide bombs fitted with 11-second delay fuses, four of which struck the main runway. Aungban, Heho and Kunlon airfields were subsequently targeted by Mosquitos from the unit, with 16 500-lb bombs being dropped from 10,000 ft down to 6000 ft and four more expended from 'zero feet'.

The new batch of delayed-action bomb fuses were still unpredictable, with virtually instantaneous detonation at times. Furthermore, releasing the bombs from low-level sometimes caused them to 'skip', as Flg Off Doug Goodrich explained. 'On many occasions bombs were seen to bounce off the ground to a greater height than that of the aircraft which had dropped them.' If the time delay was not sufficient, these 'bouncers' could be close to the Mosquito that had dropped them when they airburst.

On 4 February, No 45 Sqn's Flg Off Pete Ewing RAAF and WO Robert 'Pinkie' Pinkerton were tasked with performing a dawn raid on Heho airfield. During their bomb run in HR404, they saw a Ki-21 'Sally' bomber taking off. The squadron ORB recorded, 'Switching to guns, the enemy aircraft was attacked at 500 ft, fire being opened at 1,000 yards closing to 200 yards, and the enemy aircraft burst into flames and is claimed totally destroyed.'

The following day, Ewing, Pinkerton and navigator Flt Sgt Norman Smith were the ground party at Pispur range, overseeing bombing practice. Returning to base, their Jeep skidded on loose gravel and fell 15 ft into a culvert. All three were hospitalised, and sadly Smith died on 6 February.

Meanwhile, No 82 Sqn had spent several days carrying out multiple night attacks on Meiktila, Heho and Kunlon airfields, usually with 500-lb bombs. The main runway at Meiktila was hit several times.

Both Mosquito squadrons took part in an 'Earthquake' operation on 8 February – a 48-hour aerial onslaught on a key target. As well as 12 Mosquitos from each squadron, Mitchells and Thunderbolts also played their parts, all intent on neutralising the IJA's heavy artillery that was trying to dislodge the 19th Indian Infantry Division's Irrawaddy bridgehead at Singu. Kumbhirgram's station commander, Gp Capt Whiteley (formerly OC Wing HQ), led the 24 Mosquitos, each carrying their maximum 2000-lb bombload, as they targeted the IJA gun positions, causing extensive damage.

The advance on Rangoon depended upon the British Army's IV Corps crossing the Irrawaddy River. In the lead up to this event, misinformation had been passed on to the local population, some of whom were possible Japanese informers, implying that IV Corps' operation was only a limited Chindit-scale attack. Lt Gen Sir William 'Bill' Slim, commander of the Fourteenth Army, had devised the 'Extended Capital' plan that would see IV Corps move undetected down the Myittha Valley, cross the Irrawaddy and push directly on to capture the strategic base at Meiktila.

Slim's Operation *Cloak*, however, aimed to deceive the Japanese into believing that the Fourteenth Army's main objective was the city of Mandalay. IV Corps would, in fact, lead the Allied crossing of the Irrawaddy near Nyaunga and Pakokku, about 100 miles southwest of Mandalay.

On 10 February, both Nos 45 and 82 Sqns allocated four Mosquitos apiece to Operation *Cloak* to create the impression that the Allied forces were crossing the Irrawaddy River between Chauk and Yenangyaung. Under cover of darkness, each Mosquito would drop special time-delayed ordnance on the east bank of the Irrawaddy, where IV Corps wanted the Japanese to believe that the crossing was taking place.

The time-delayed ordnance (two per aircraft) was dubbed a 'battle in a canister', or a 'Parafex', which would be covertly dropped. The Mosquitos were then to continue onwards and strafe IJA lines of communication, before heading home. After a delay of one to two hours, the Parafex cannisters would activate, creating decoy 'attacks' by imitating the sound of rifle fire, punctuated by hand grenades 'exploding'. This deception was planned to occur a few days in advance of the actual crossing at Pakokku.

Eight Mosquitos sortied in two waves just before dusk, but one had to abort due to engine problems. Walsh and Orsborn, in HR567, took off at 1705 hrs. The aircraft flew independently at low-level through the darkness towards their slightly different target locations.

Approaching theirs, Walsh and Orsborn climbed up to 2500 ft to drop their Parafex. After releasing them, they 'experienced a total electrics failure'. Without their radio, electrical instruments or even the navigator's map light, Walsh decided against strafing. With no electrics, at night and in deteriorating weather, they headed north for home. Walsh recalled;

'Believing we had dropped the Parafex on target, we endeavoured to make our way back to base without a radio. Needless to say, with no moon, flooding and swollen rivers and increasingly high cumulus, especially over the mountains, we got hopelessly lost and were very low on fuel. We were almost at the point of bailing out when, by a sheer stroke of luck, we spotted the lights of a very small landing strip.

'We made an emergency landing (downwind as it happens) on a short strip. The plane overshot the lights and ploughed through a burnt-out Dakota. This forward landing strip was Onbauk, near

New Zealander Flt Lt Rex Garnham and his navigator, Australian Flt Lt Jack Nankervis, pose for an RNZAF photographer on two 500-lb bombs loaded on a trolley at Kumbhirgram on 7 January 1945 (*RNZAF Official PR4867*)

Mandalay, and Jap forces were all around it, often attacking it at night with mortar and machine-gun fire.'

Once they were out of their Mosquito, Walsh and Orsborn realised that it 'was badly damaged, and because of the electrics failure, we found the Parafex still on board!' Some Americans soon drove up in an unlit Jeep and shouted at them to get in. As they climbed into the Jeep, IJA troops started shooting. 'The Yanks gave us a lift back in their Jeep, and that was more frightening than any flight.' The next day, the crew hitched a lift to the airfield at Shwebo. There, they 'got transport to Imphal and then back to base'.

The following night, eight more Parafexes were expended. Having dropped their canisters, Flg Off Rex Garnham RNZAF and Flt Lt Jack 'Nank' Nankervis RAAF started strafing roads and railways, before taking in the airfields of Allanmyo and Magwe. However, AA fire was accurate at Magwe and their aircraft was sufficiently damaged for them to complete a precautionary landing at Kalemyo. The final Parafexes were dropped by No 82 Sqn on 14 February.

The deception was soon found to have worked, for when the real crossing at Pagan was launched a day or so later, many IJA troops had been drawn further south. Although the Japanese soldiers left behind defended their positions 'fanatically', the rout of the IJA's 15th Army had begun. Soon, Slim's Fourteenth Army effectively controlled the western bank of the Irrawaddy to a point 30 miles south of the confluence with the Chindwin.

To aid the advance, Mosquitos provided effective ground support further south and east to the Sittang River. Until the aircraft could be moved south from Kumbhirgram, they used a recently opened Advanced Landing Ground at Thazi, to the east of the Chin Hills, after British Army engineers quickly created a 6900-ft runway. The Mosquitos would use it both day and night, even though runway lighting was described as 'minimal'. Thazi acted as an intermediate refuelling point that allowed crews to top up on their way to or returning from their targets. Either option would allow them to continue to carry four 500-lb bombs. It also enabled longer-range 'rhubarbs' and strafing with full bomb loads.

With little chance of rest and relaxation in Kumbhirgram's jungle setting, the strain of intruder flying – hours of intense concentration, inherent danger and proximity with death – started showing in different ways. Some aircrew resisted forming new friendships, others experienced more frequent nightmares, and nervous afflictions dubbed 'the twitch' were relatively common.

As a remedy, squadron commanders ensured that aircrew took their annual leave. Wg Cdr Snell and his navigator Flg Off Arthur Maude were given a week off operations in February, whilst Flt Lts Duclos and MacFadzean had 14 days' leave starting on 2 February. Then, WO Walsh and Flt Sgt Orsborn went to Calcutta for leave towards the end of the month. They had taken advantage of an aircrew perk that meant they could hitch a lift in No 45 Sqn's twin-engined Expeditor II communications aircraft to RAF Baigachi, near Calcutta, saving them three days of travel each way. Having completed their three-year overseas tours with the RAF, Australian crews started returning home at this time too, replaced by Mosquito crews from Britain.

With Flg Off Ewing still recovering from the Jeep crash on 5 February, WO Pinkerton, now fit to fly, was temporarily paired up with pilot

Mosquito FB VI TA477/UX-F of No 82 Sqn receives attention from barechested groundcrew at Kumbhirgram in early 1945. Much of the fin has been stripped of paint and the wing leading edge also shows signs of having been recently worked on. The aircraft's weight is being born by two jacks, which suggests that the undercarriage has also been checked (*Philip Jarrett Collection*)

Flt Sgt Gordon Ashworth. On 17 February they were one of six crews tasked with bombing IJAAF airfields in central Burma, taking off just before 0400 hrs. Ashworth and Pinkerton were allocated Heho airfield as a target, and their aircraft was armed with two 500-lb bombs, plus cannon and machine gun rounds. Whilst the remaining five crews returned safely from their sorties, there was no sign of Ashworth and Pinkerton. Wg Cdr Walker despatched Flg Off McLellan and Flt Lt Jim Vernon RAAF to search, in vain, for any signs of them or their aircraft. Ashworth and Pinkerton were duly posted 'Missing, believed killed'.

Four No 82 Sqn crews were tasked with dawn 'rhubarbs' on 19 February. Despatched first was Plt Off Thynne, with WO Bill Flatt navigating, taking off at 0458 hrs in HR228. Immediately, something went tragically wrong, the Mosquito crashing into trees just 1500 yards beyond the end of the runway and exploding in flames.

Later that same day, Flg Off Alfred 'Mac' McKenzie RAAF and navigator Flt Lt R K Pears were tasked with leading a Mosquito pair to 'rhubarb' the road and railway from Mandalay to Lashio. WO R W Murkin, with navigator Flt Sgt Charles Carruthers RAAF, who had only arrived a week earlier, flew the second aircraft. After avoiding heavily defended Mandalay, they started following the railway line south, as Carruthers recalled;

'Everything was going quite well and I was keeping a wary eye on our tail for "Oscars" – those nasty little Jap fighters. After a quarter-of-an-hour or so, we spotted a loco in a bamboo hut (the Japs' poor attempt at camouflage). This we strafed, and saw dust and possible steam rising from it. Proceeding happily up the railway line, weaving from side to side, suddenly the sky was filled with little black puffs of smoke. They looked quite harmless, but knowing what Bofors can do caused us no little anxiety. Our nose went down immediately – throttles open – and we left at great speed. Having thought we were out of range, I glanced behind and was shaken to see those little black puffs following closely on our tail.'

McKenzie initially thought his Mosquito had been hit, but his aircraft seemed fine, so both crews continued with the 'rhubarb'. Having found the road south, they started to patrol it. 'Then, like a bolt from the blue, we heard "Mac" yell, "Bandits – for God's sake open her out!"', Carruthers continued. 'So once again down went the nose and throttles through the gate this time, and we hurtled along at a steady 350 mph right on the deck. It didn't take us long to outrun them.'

Suspecting that other fighters might be in the area, the two crews headed west, hoping that the danger was now behind them. However, according to Carruthers;

'Then a further "Oscar" was sighted, which caused us great alarm as he appeared to be turning in to attack us. This time it was not so easy, as we were flying at about 50 ft and right in front of us was a range of mountains. Somehow, we managed to top the rise, and screamed down the other side approaching the 400-mph mark. The old Merlins were "dragging at their anchors" and the whole kite was shuddering. This was the least of our worries, and we finally reached our lines and set course for base. We landed okay after four hours of very exciting and nerve-wracking experiences.'

No 82 Sqn's FB VI RF784/UX-N was one of the first Mosquitos to be operated by the unit in the new reflective silver finish adopted in-theatre. It also had definitive SEAC theatre recognition markings. The aircraft was photographed from a second silver Mosquito during a mission in February–March 1945. RF784 was later passed on to No 47 Sqn when No 82 Sqn disbanded in March 1946 (*Philip Jarrett Collection*)

Having received its first Mosquitos in mid-February, No 47 Sqn's 'A' Flight pressed ahead with conversion. Plt Off Bob Willis, with his navigator Plt Off Tommy Thompson, quickly transitioned from the Beaufighter to the Mosquito. 'Tommy and I were allocated Mosquito HR518 "D for Dog", which was to prove an exceptionally reliable aircraft,' Willis explained. 'The aircraft in their new reflective silver paint, instead of European-style camouflage, and with inspection panels installed gave us total confidence that we had a first-class machine to fly.'

Willis and Thompson duly flew No 47 Sqn's first Mosquito operation on 23 February, paired for a daylight 'rhubarb' with Flt Lt Bill Bailey and WO F W Poree. Due to a shortage of Mosquito drop tanks, their aircraft were equipped with a long-range 63-gallon fuel tank in the bomb-bay. Willis continued;

'We flew from Kumbhirgram over the Chin Hills at 10,000 ft, skirting the mountains to the East of Mandalay at Maymyo, then southwest to Kyaukse on the main railway line 30 miles south of Mandalay. Continuing south, we had reasonable success on this 4 hr 20 min sortie, catching and strafing a locomotive in sheds at Pyananggazu, 30 miles east of Meiktila.'

A further six weeks would pass before No 47 Sqn completed its conversion from the Beaufighter X to the Mosquito FB VI.

On 25 February, according to No 82 Sqn's ORB, Sqn Ldr Albert Tooth, with navigator WO George Tippett RAAF, 'were jumped by an "Oscar", which shot away their elevator cables'. Tooth was forced to return to base controlling HR406's elevators via the trim tabs only. He eventually brought the aircraft in to land at Kumbhirgram, wheels up, at 200 mph. Medical officer Flt Lt Dawes described it as 'a spectacular but terrifying exhibition. Sqn Ldr Tooth was completely unmoved by the event. This officer is one of the most fearless – and ruthless – men I have ever met, and is a very great asset to the squadron'.

Flt Lt Vic Hewes and navigator Sgt Gordon Thewlis had recently joined No 82 Sqn. Having flown their first Mosquito intruder sortie the day prior to Tooth's high-speed landing, an operation targeted through intelligence from Force 136 (a small team from the Special Operations Executive working behind enemy lines) followed on 26 February. Force 136 had identified that the IJA was hiding medical supplies destined for troops of

33rd Division under hay on bullock carts – they were monitoring a convoy of carts making its way north towards the frontline.

Hewes and Thewlis took off at dawn from Thazi and headed southeast, the latter recalling;

'The target given to us was Ywadon, but the bullock cart convoy had moved on a little by the time we arrived there. After a few moments searching in the general direction they were heading, we spotted them in line astern, about eight of them in total, edging along a narrow track banking alongside rice paddy fields. Making a broadside approach, we hit the first two, then made a steep turn to port and made a similar attack on the rear three, finishing off the trapped middle three with a third strafing.'

Thewlis took no pleasure in these attacks;

'Our ammunition belts on both the 0.303-cal. Browning machine guns and the 20 mm Hispano cannon had been loaded with extra incendiary bullets and shells to cause the most effective damage. Flame- and smoke-damaged medical supplies would be of little use. The horrifying part was seeing the bullocks in the shafts falling to the ground, having been hit with either stray bullets or shells. It was also unfortunate for the Burmese Teamsters who were caught up in the attacks. They had probably been drafted into this job under duress by their Japanese conquerors. My conscience didn't play any part at this point, but we did come to realise that this was the horror of war at close hand.

'On all these low-level sorties the cockpit became hot, with sweat stinging the eyes and the body saturated with perspiration. Such conditions, combined with the sticky, acrid smell of cordite fumes, made these missions a very unpleasant and unforgettable experience.'

Such sorties were both stressful and exhausting, with the continuous turbulence of flying low over dense jungle and the heat and noise generated by a pair of Merlins bellowing away on either side of the cockpit. Physically drained, Hewes and Thewlis were forced to land at Thazi due to cloud over the Manipur Mountains. According to Thewlis;

'Had the weather been clear, I doubt if we could have made it to our home base. Perhaps God was on our side clamping down the weather. As it was, we were diverted again from Thazi to Imphal because of bad weather, eventually leaving there for Kumbhirgram [on 27 February]. All in all, this operation had taken nearly two days to complete. It was then debriefing and off to bed to recover.'

On the last day of the month, Willis and Thompson of No 47 Sqn took part in a two-ship night 'rhubarb' led by the new 'A' Flight commander, Flt Lt Al Scott RCAF. After clearing the Chin Hills, the two aircraft went their separate ways, with Willis and Thompson following the railway line from Meiktila towards Rangoon. After attacking a locomotive at Kume Road, light AA fire opened up, but they escaped and returned towards Thazi. According to Willis;

'Landing at Thazi at night was far from easy, with the strip sloping away as you touched down. We approached the runway in a long and steady descent, not daring to overshoot, touching down as close as possible to the Chance Light [named after its manufacturer, Chance Brothers] situated to the right at the near end of the strip [illuminating the runway threshold]. The landing lights in the wings were fully on. As soon as the pilot could see the ground from the illumination of his landing lights, then it was time to level off and effect a landing.'

On arrival, they arranged refuelling and bedded down for the night;

'If staying overnight, it was in tented accommodation, hoping to find a spare camp bed on which to snatch a few hours' sleep, still in full flying clothing. Breakfast would be lots of tea and probably fried Spam, before taking off for base and debriefing.'

Sadly, two of No 45 Sqn's new replacement aircrew did not see the month out. That same day (28 February), Flt Lt Brian Draper and WO Peter James were killed during a bombing attack on a concentration of IJA troops and armour near Sedaw when HR457 broke up at about 4000 ft in a dive. Flg Off McLellan was flying the following aircraft;

'We were doing some shallow dive-bombing attacks on Jap positions when the aircraft preceding us broke up in a shower of confetti. That may have happened with other crews and never been witnessed.'

Clearly the Mosquito's airframe problems were not fully resolved. WO Sinclair 'Tiff' O'Connor also had his own aircraft-related problems on this operation. He and WO Anthony McKie, in HR462, had a bomb that would not release, O'Connor recalling, 'We had several cases on Mosquitos, fortunately always with wing bombs that tended to fall off on the final approach after all previous efforts to dislodge them had failed. We discovered that they fell off when the flaps were lowered – a jettison procedure! All the armourers insisted that an "open hook" hang-up was impossible. My port wing bomb hung-up, but fortunately it fell in a ravine on the approach to Kumbhirgram, so we escaped the major part of the blast.'

MARCH 1945

With monsoon season approaching, it became hotter and hazier. March started disastrously for No 82 Sqn. With bad weather at Kumbhirgram, on the first day of the month, the unit was forced to fly sorties from Thazi against the airfields at Pyinmana and Toungoo. At 2115 hrs, tasked with attacking Pyinmana, Plt Off David Kinnell started his take-off run in HR458 and had barely completed 100 yards when his Mosquito inexplicably swung off the runway. The aircraft ran into cattle, turned over and immediately burst into flames. Both Kinnell and his navigator, WO Harry Lambert, were killed. The bursting of a tyre had caused the crash.

Just three hours later, at 0015 hrs on 2 March, WO Robert Best and his navigator, Flt Sgt Andrew Lorimer, took off in HR439 to attack Toungoo. Sadly, they too were killed in a crash near Rangoon.

Most operational sorties now used Thazi as their start point. On 4 March, eight of No 45 Sqn's crews were detached there in the late afternoon. After resting for a few hours, they began preparing for their mission just after midnight. At 0140 hrs on the 5th, WO O'Connor had just started to accelerate for take-off in HR404 when a water buffalo ran across the runway. His Mosquito was destroyed and the buffalo killed, but luckily both he and WO McKie were able to walk away from the crash. Thazi was temporarily closed.

Regardless of the deteriorating weather, the Fourteenth Army continued to advance on the strategically important town of Meiktila. After days of heavy fighting, it was taken on 4 March, only for the IJA to then succeed in surrounding the Allied troops. For days, all supplies had to be ferried in by air, and the British Army's grip on the town and nearby airfield remained precarious, with aircraft often flying in and out during enemy mortar attacks.

Having tried to rest through the evening of 7 March, WO Walsh reported to the flight hut after midnight to prepare for his next operation, scheduled for the early hours of the 8th. Ten aircraft from No 45 Sqn were tasked with attacking four IJAAF airfields – Heho, Tougoo, Pyinmana and Tennant. Walsh and his navigator, Flt Sgt Orsborn, were one of three crews tasked with glide-bombing Pyinmana airfield, about 100 miles south of Mandalay, with two 500-lb instant-fused weapons.

The three aircraft took off at about 90-minute intervals, flying as singletons to ensure that the airfield attacks were well separated. The weather was not great, requiring crews to fly for over an hour on instruments. However, Walsh and Orsborn found their target before dawn, completed the attack and noted that a 'skeleton flarepath was lit'. They then patrolled the airfield for a while but did not see any activity. They subsequently landed at Kumbhirgram at 0645 hrs, drained from the concentration required during the four-and-a-half-hour night and instrument sortie. Thinking of breakfast and sleep after debriefing, Walsh and Orsborn were surprised when they were told to report back to the flight hut at midday. They had been rostered to fly again that afternoon.

The morning of 8 March also saw six aircraft from No 82 Sqn tasked with bombing the Pyinmana railway bypass bridge over the Sittang River. The operation was led by unit CO Wg Cdr 'Freddy' Snell, with Flg Off Maude navigating, in HR497. Two of the other crews were Flt Lts Dick 'Scotty' McKenzie and Ray Pears in HR545 and Flg Off Wambeek and WO Mooney in HR311. They took off from Kumbhirgram at 0730 hrs in fine but slightly hazy weather. Following their return, the squadron ORB noted;

'All aircraft dropped bombs close to the target without actually hitting the bridge. All bombs were near misses and the bridge may have been damaged by blast but crews do not report any visible damage.'

That only told part of the story. Snell made his bombing run at 50 ft, and as he released his ordnance, a very heavy explosion occurred beneath the aircraft, with debris flung violently against it, injuring Maude. The CO believed a land mine had detonated as the Mosquito flew over it. Flt Lt Dawes reported;

'A stone thrown upwards by the force of the explosion penetrated the undersurface of the aircraft and pierced the navigator's seat. W/Cdr Snell very wisely administered a Tubunic ampoule of morphia, which relieved symptoms and resulted in the navigator falling asleep.'

Again according to the ORB, 'the fuselage [of HR497] from nose to tail was riddled with holes and mainplanes and tailplanes were likewise riddled with holes – a huge gaping hole had been torn in the Browning machine gun stowage in the nose'. Maude's injuries kept him out of action for six weeks.

Having bombed the bridge, McKenzie, with Wambeek as his wingman, swept low over the nearby Lew II airstrip in the hope of catching some IJAAF fighters on the ground. The airfield's AA batteries were waiting, however, as Wambeek explained. 'My port engine was struck and streamed glycol, intercom with my navigator, Brian Mooney, ceased and it became apparent that our hydraulics were damaged.'

With the port propeller feathered, and after initially setting course for Sadaung some 200 miles to the north, it became clear they would not make it. McKenzie and Pears stayed with Wambeek and Mooney, recognising their plight. At briefing they had been told that, in an emergency, they could use Meiktila. Wambeek continued;

'The instructions must have been intended for the single-engined fighter-bombers that were giving close support to our ground forces. Now, with one engine feathered and the radiator temperature off the clock, our chances of reaching our own lines were slender.'

Descending from 2000 ft, the haze obscured Wambeek's visibility. Having lowered his undercarriage, suddenly a Dakota threw up a dust cloud as it started to take off, 'completely obliterating my view of the strip. Seconds later, on checking, I found that my starboard wheel was hanging down, but not locked, and my port wheel remained locked up'.

Still having sufficient height and airspeed from his one remaining engine, Wambeek diverted to Meiktila's small satellite strip about seven miles southeast. 'It appeared out of the haze sooner than expected, and I throttled back and shoved the nose down, but with no flaps my speed built up rapidly.' He unbuckled his harness to unfeather his port propeller and his Mosquito crossed the airfield boundary at 185 mph, with the rough grass strip only 700–800 yards in length and a steam roller, left of centre, two-thirds of the way down.

Having cut the remaining fuel cock and ignition switches, he threw his left arm across the gunsight and slid forward on the seat, resting his face on his other arm, braced against the rudder pedals and eased the control column forward. After impact, they seemed to be aiming for the steam roller until, at the last minute, the Mosquito slewed around to a halt, breaking in two. Mooney was trapped in his seat but, like Wambeek, he too was unharmed. Then they heard McKenzie on the radio, yelling 'Get out of that aircraft bloody quick'. They had soon clambered out of the top hatch, hoping that McKenzie would get a message to troops in the immediate area. They waited in the scrub, the air thick with the sickly stench from more than 4000 rotting bodies following the Battle of Meiktila, and about two hours later they were picked up by an army patrol and taken to the main airfield.

Just four hours after their debriefing, Walsh and Orsborn were back in the flight hut being briefed on attacking the Pyinmana bridges, flying as wingmen to the CO, Wg Cdr Walker, and his navigator, Flt Lt Frank Harper. At 1345 hrs the Mosquito pair took off, heading to the south of the Meiktila junction. After nearly two hours of flying at low-level through the heat of the afternoon, they arrived at their primary target to find that one span on the main bridge was already down. They immediately focused on bombing its bypass bridge.

The CO completed his glide attack at 320 mph and his bombs landed just to the east of the bridge. A large blue flash was seen

Thwatti railway bridge was frequently attacked, together with the bypass line and the bridge alongside it. This photograph of the severed lines, a downed bridge and bomb-cratered land surrounding the target area was taken by a low-flying No 45 Sqn Mosquito on 9 March 1945 (*Author's Collection*)

about a quarter-of-a-mile from the southwest end of the main bridge, the blast rocking Walker's Mosquito and causing temporary failure of his elevator control. Walker thought it could have been a land mine, as had happened to Wg Cdr Snell earlier in the day near the same bridge. This was possibly a new IJA tactic against the low-flying Mosquitos.

The two aircraft then followed the railway north towards another of the secondary targets. As soon as Orsborn identified Sinthe railway bridge, Walsh started his attack run with a slightly slower approach to increase accuracy, putting his Mosquito into a shallow glide attack at 275 mph. He released his four 500-lb bombs from 400 ft onto the bridge, tearing up the railway line. Both crews then 'rhubarbed' their way north, with Walsh claiming a train damaged. They landed safely back at base at 1748 hrs as dusk fell, with Walsh and Orsborn now truly exhausted.

Three days later, on 11 March, 13 Mosquitos and crews from No 110 Sqn flew from RAF Yelahanka directly to RAF Joari, near Cox's Bazar, having finally completed their training on the aircraft – the unit's conversion from the Vengeance to the FB VI had started several months earlier. However, the armourers and ground support had to make their way by train and truck, which would take many days.

The CO of No 47 Sqn, Wg Cdr William 'Billy' Filson-Young, also undertook his first operation in a Mosquito from Kumbhirgram on 11 March. Until then, he had continued to fly missions in the Beaufighter. The squadron's Mosquitos were fitted with rocket projectile rails so that they could continue using RP-3s (a favourite weapon for Beaufighters in-theatre) for ground attack. At 1019 hrs, Filson-Young took off, together with Plt Off Bob Willis in a second Mosquito, to 'rhubarb' the roads along the Irrawaddy. The aircraft scored hits on three open trucks, although both Mosquitos were also damaged by AA fire during their four-hour operation.

On 15 March, Nos 45 and 82 Sqns collaborated on a joint operation using 24 Mosquitos to attack the oil installations at Yenangyaung. Timed to arrive over the target at 1300 hrs, the No 82 Sqn aircraft would deliver their bombs in a shallow-dive attack from 12,000 ft, whilst No 45 Sqn's Mosquitos approached from the east at low-level in line abreast with 11-second time delay fuses fitted to their ordnance.

As No 45 Sqn flew in at about 300 mph at 50 ft, some aircraft started to draw ahead of four others, including Flg Off McLellan and Flt Lt Vernon in HR451. The time delay on their colleagues' bombs did not work, as McLellan recalled;

'Over the target, the whole ground came up to meet us as 32 500-lb bombs dropped by the preceding aircraft exploded together. We seemed to be flying through solid earth mixed with all sorts of junk from trees to 40-gallon drums. The noise was mind bending, and holes, large and small, appeared everywhere in the aircraft. A black log about six feet long hung suspended perpendicularly in the air in front of me, but there was nothing I could do to avoid it. We hit it with a terrific bang, which yawed the aircraft. The log jammed in the leading edge of the wing between me and the port motor and stayed there against the main spar. This was not a good thing, as the leading edge also contained the oil radiator for that engine, and oil was pouring out of it. At the same time, every Jap gun was concentrating on us, and we could feel the thuds of hits and hear the explosions. I had accepted that this was the end but felt quite calm.

'We were really shot up by 40 mm flak, and I had six feet of teak log jammed in my port oil radiator – the engine consequently seized. In addition, I had a 500-lb fused bomb hanging on an open hook in the bomb-bay. The starboard engine was overheating, and I could not get above 1000 ft with 500 miles to go to the nearest advanced fighter strip. I was waiting for the glycol in the starboard engine to blow off, so I told Jim, my navigator, to bail out, and I would follow. He refused to go, insisting that I was competent to complete a belly landing in the river!'

McLellan and Vernon set course for the airstrip at Kalewa, but they still had about 100 miles to go when, quite by chance, they found the newly opened Thunderbolt strip at Sinthe;

'We were still arguing amicably when the fighter strip came into view, and I landed from a righthand circuit, cursing a "Dak" which was in its landing circuit ahead of us. With the aid of the handpump, we had enough hydraulic pressure to lock the undercart as we touched down, but did not have enough pressure to put down the flaps. The coolant blew off in the starboard engine during our approach. Without flaps, we were doing 100 mph without brakes when we came to the end of the strip on rough ground.'

The Mosquito ploughed through storage areas and, undercarriage collapsed, slid to a halt on its belly;

'Happily, the hung-up bomb in the bomb-bay did not explode. The good old "Mossie" did bring us home, or nearly home, on every operation. The aircraft did not get us back to base on this occasion, but we were down in friendly territory.'

On 16 March, the convoy of groundcrew and equipment for No 110 Sqn finally departed on its way to Joari. However, it would take 11 more days to reach the unit, further delaying the start of operations. Squadron CO, Wg Cdr Saunders, was unimpressed. 'It would appear that little or no organisation was made for the transfer of the squadron equipment onwards to Joari from Calcutta. This is being referred to higher authority.'

The intruders' tasking now focused on cutting off the IJA's retreat, as well as its supply lines. With Mosquitos being serviced and re-armed as quickly as possible, units were now delivering more than 25 sorties each day. On 20 March, the Fourteenth Army's flag was raised above the walls of Mandalay's Fort Dufferin.

Five days later, No 45 Sqn's CO, Wg Cdr Walker, flew another sortie in HR627 with his navigator, Flt Lt Harper, taking off at 0655 hrs to attack an important bridge over the Sittang River at Toungoo. The target was well defended, and Walker made several runs over it before releasing his bombs. He then returned to secure a

The oil storage facilities at Yenaungyan were also routinely targeted by Mosquitos throughout the campaign. No 47 Sqn aircraft were responsible for this particular attack on 27 March 1945 (*SWWEC – LEEWW.2008.085 Bailey, D A*)

photograph of the results. It was at this point that HR627 was hit by AA fire, smashing the bullet-proof windscreen in front of him. Walker was cut about the eyes, temporarily blinded and lost consciousness. Harper immediately unbuckled himself, leaned over his CO and took control of the aircraft, flying clear of the target.

When Walker came round, Harper gave him first aid and staunched the flow of blood. Meiktila refused them permission to land. However, with shepherding from wingmen Sqn Ldr George Dyke and WO 'Joe' Zussen, Harper and his badly wounded pilot managed to fly their damaged aircraft to Monywa. After two aborted landing attempts, they touched down successfully at 1030 hrs. Walker was transferred to hospital in Comilla, where surgeons were able to save the sight in both eyes, although one had permanently impaired vision. Having completed 53 Mosquito intruder operations, Wg Cdr Walker was repatriated to Britain. He was later awarded the Distinguished Service Order. Sqn Ldr Duclos was immediately appointed as the new CO.

On 26 March, two No 45 Sqn Mosquitos departed Kumbhirgram at 0415 hrs to patrol the Toungoo–Pyinmana area, arriving at 0615 hrs. WO Alan Holmes, with navigator Sgt William Austen, flying HR527, sighted two vehicles near Toungoo and attacked them, scoring hits on one. Unfortunately, the aircraft failed to pull out of its dive and crashed, bursting into flames upon hitting the ground.

Despite such losses, the Mosquito intruders continued delivering a maximum effort. Three days later, No 82 Sqn recorded the loss of another aircraft, HR489. Although Flg Off Gwilym Hayes and Sgt Ronald Black radioed to say that they were abandoning their burning aircraft, neither of them got out before it crashed near Allagappa.

The tasking peaked at the end of the month. Flt Sgt Alf Pridmore recalled the operations that he and his pilot, Flg Off Don Blenkhorne, flew at this time;

'On the 30th, the first sortie was flown at 0655 [hrs] in Mosquito HR368 [to Loikaw road bridge], and it lasted four hours. After a brief rest, the second sortie [to a road bridge southwest of Ywashhit] began at 1400 [hrs] and ended almost four hours later! With a little rest, the next sortie was flown [to Loikaw road bridge again] at 0720 [hrs] the following morning. On all of these sorties the targets were damaged.'

On 31 March, ten No 45 Sqn Mosquitos were tasked with an early morning attack on road and rail bridges. Walsh and Orsborn were ordered to hit a road bridge to the east of Toungoo, more than 120 miles south of Meiktila. Setting off just after 0700 hrs, immediately Walsh realised they had a problem with their wing-mounted bombs, so he jettisoned them. Since they still had two 500-lb 11-second delay weapons in their bomb-bay, they continued with the raid. The bridge was attacked from low-level, with both bombs on target. However, the target was not destroyed.

Walsh then dropped the Mosquito to treetop height to 'rhubarb' any traffic on the roads and railway line north as they returned to Kumbhirgram. Following a gruelling 4 hr 20 min sortie, Walsh and Orsborn handed their aircraft back to groundcrew, who immediately started to service, refuel and rearm it. The squadron was now very short of serviceable aircraft, and eight of the ten Mosquitos from the morning op were used again that afternoon.

At Joari, determined to start operations during March, Wg Cdr Saunders arranged for two crews to fly ops on the last day of the month. Finally, No 110 Sqn's Mosquitos were operational.

During March, No 45 Sqn dropped 556,500 lbs of bombs – more than during its entire 16 months of flying Vengeances. Supplies of replacement Mosquitos had dried up. Spare parts were scavenged from crashed aircraft, and the unit had even started scrapping Mosquitos rather than servicing them. Recently promoted Wg Cdr Duclos, No 45 Sqn's new CO, had only 13 serviceable Mosquitos. He reported that, 'unless the supply position improves, we shall be very short indeed'. He also noted the aircrew disapproval of the silver-doped Mosquitos;

'Whatever the technical advantage of this scheme may be, and it is considered to be very limited, the operational disadvantages incurred are considerable.'

Wg Cdr Snell, CO of No 82 Sqn, echoed the concerns about aircraft;

'The large number of hours flown this month, although excellent in its way, has put a great strain on the replacement situation in the rear areas, with a consequent drop in serviceability which may be felt for some time.'

APRIL 1945

Despite the IJA retreat, Field Marshal Slim feared that the Japanese would defend Rangoon to the last man, so he reinstated Operation *Dracula* – the airborne and amphibious assault on the Burmese capital. The Allied advance southwards had to continue.

March had been a punishing month for No 45 Sqn's aircrew, so, on 2 April, Wg Cdr Duclos arranged a much needed 48-hour stand-down. Pilots and navigators caught up on some rest and the engineers returned two more aircraft to serviceable status.

Operations resumed on the morning of 4 April, with six aircraft flying sorties. In the afternoon, Walsh and Orsborn were one of four No 45 Sqn crews tasked with attacking Zinga village, which the IJA was using as a military base. They would be flying the final aircraft in the attack, and had been allocated HR567, recently returned to the squadron after they had crashed it on 10 February. In the early afternoon, Walsh and Orsborn walked out to HR567, now repainted with the silver dope. Although this colour scheme made the aircraft more vulnerable for night operations, Walsh was not particularly concerned, for he felt that the silver could be useful with their task that day as they would be attacking out of the setting sun.

Their Mosquito had been armed with two 500-lb high-explosive bombs and two 500-lb incendiaries. As soon as they were settled in the stiflingly hot cockpit, they ran their pre-start checks. Walsh fired up the two Merlins, checked temperatures and pressures and, with a green light from the watch tower, immediately taxied to the runway holding point. The first leg of their sortie was the familiar transit over the Manipur Range and then south to their landing strip at Thazi. Once parked up, the aircraft were handed over to the groundcrew, who set about refuelling the Mosquitos ready for the main part of the operation itself. Having found some shade from the afternoon sun, the four crews finalised tactics.

Zinga was a further 200 miles south along the Sittang River valley. However, to ensure surprise, the Mosquito crews would separate into pairs and aim to arrive at dusk for a coordinated attack on the village. Walsh and Orsborn would follow a route that would take about 1 hr 40 min to fly. They would drop down to low-level behind the Pegu Yoma hills, on the eastern side of the Irrawaddy River valley. They watched as the first pair departed down the strip from Thazi, then they fired up HR567 and taxied to the holding point, accompanied by HR332 flown by Flg Offs Freddie Fortune and Joe Mears.

The Mosquito pair headed southwest, initially following the Chindwin River. South of Monywa, they changed course towards Meiktila and then flew south along the western side of the Pegu Yoma. They were now on maximum alert, scanning for fighters from the still active IJAAF airfields. They remained at low-level throughout, even though such a flight profile consumed more fuel. Having identified the ground feature for their attack run on Zinga, they set off over the Pegu Yoma hills and across the Sittang River floodplain.

With Fortune leading them towards the village, fires were evident from the previous Mosquito attacks. Walsh positioned his aircraft for their attack run, dropping the incendiaries and high explosives and strafing the village with cannon and machine gun fire. Fifty years later, Walsh dispassionately recalled the attack. 'As the evening light began to fade, we ran in to bomb Zinga village and, as we left the target, it appeared that it had been accurately hit.' Their mission was accomplished, for they had left the village burning.

With darkness falling, the four Mosquitos cleared the mountains to the east of the Sittang River valley and headed north, remaining at low-level. Breaking radio silence, Fortune told Walsh that his airspeed indicator had failed, making navigation difficult and landing hazardous. Walsh immediately adopted the role of 'shepherd', with Fortune in loose formation on him. The return trip in the dark would take longer because Walsh and Orsborn could not risk losing Fortune and Mears.

As time passed, Orsborn became increasingly concerned with their aircraft's unusually high fuel consumption. He and Walsh considered their options, concluding that their best and possibly only choice was to try to make it to Monywa, which could light up a flarepath for them. Walsh climbed the Mosquito to 5000 ft, with Fortune shadowing him, and then set it up for maximum endurance. They called for a QDM (an emergency magnetic homing) to Monywa, advising the airfield that they would need an 'immediate landing'.

They started descending as soon as they could see Monywa's flarepath. With little fuel left, Walsh flew a direct approach, with Fortune close behind, relying on Walsh to keep to the right airspeed. Approaching the flarepath, Walsh ran his landing checks, selected flaps, lowered the undercarriage and switched on the landing lights. As he continued his final approach to the runway threshold, his aircraft's lights revealed the runway already below them. To his horror, Walsh realised that Monywa had only lit a flarepath long enough for the Hurricanes based there. Even worse, the flarepath was at the far end of the runway. With Fortune's Mosquito a few seconds behind them, they did not have any options other than to land.

'BRACE, "OSSIE", BRACE', Walsh shouted as he touched the Mosquito down at just over 120 mph at the start of the flarepath, switched off the fuel, throttled back the engines and started applying the brakes.

He and Orsborn prepared themselves for the inevitable crash, as well as a possible impact from Fortune's Mosquito. As they went off the end of the runway and continued into the darkness, barbed wire at the airfield perimeter tangled with the turning propellers and flailed the nose and cockpit of their aircraft. Then they hit an AA gun position which ripped off the Mosquito's undercarriage. Fortune's Mosquito could not avoid hitting them, ripping off its undercarriage during the impact.

Suddenly, there was near silence, apart from the ticking of the hot engines. Released from their seats and their parachute harnesses, Walsh and Orsborn scrambled to get out of their Mosquito through the exit hatch in the cockpit canopy. They climbed out onto the wing root and clambered down to the ground. There was no fire, but there was no time to hang around with hot engines, fuel and a damaged aircraft made of wood. As they jogged away from their aircraft, they checked with Fortune and Mears. Incredibly, no one had been hurt, even in the gun position. Both HR567 and HR332 were total write-offs, further reducing No 45 Sqn's capabilities.

At Joari, No 110 Sqn was settling into the rhythm of operational flying, with two Mosquito pairs tasked on both 1 and 2 April, increasing to three pairs on each of the next three days. On the 6th, three pairs were again tasked but, sadly, Flt Lt Bernard Findlay and Flg Off Lawrence Hurst failed to return from their road and rail reconnaissance mission from Pegu to Martaban. They were No 110 Sqn's first operational losses with the Mosquito.

The intruder Mosquitos' tasking was changing, and now it involved destroying enemy fuel and supply dumps, as well as troop concentrations and railways. On both 5 and 6 April, No 45 Sqn attacked the railway station at Hngettheik, then six aircraft took out an ammunition and supply dump at Pasawng. However, after the total commitment in March, the unit rarely managed to exceed eight sorties a day. Even the few replacement aircraft received often required work before operational use.

A formation of seven silver-painted FB VIs from No 45 Sqn, photographed from an eighth Mosquito in April–May 1945. Such numbers were rarely seen in the same patch of sky during combat operations in the Far East, squadrons usually only sending out Mosquitos in pairs or as four-ship formations (*SWWEC – LEEWW.2001.1762 White, G W*)

No 47 Sqn continued with its conversion from Beaufighters to Mosquitos, increasing the number of daily FB VI sorties to eight. Again, fuel dumps, bridges and troop concentrations were their targets. On 12 April, squadron CO Wg Cdr Filson-Young led three other Mosquitos in an attack on a reported enemy troop build-up near Allanmyo. Having strafed their primary target, they then attacked an oil pipeline and three camouflaged oil tanks at Minbu.

Two days later, a pair of No 47 Sqn Mosquitos were tasked with strafing a fuel dump at Toungoo, close to a reported IJA rest camp. The mission was very successful, with three bashas (bamboo huts) left on fire and black smoke rising to 1500 ft. During the attack, the port engine of the Mosquito flown by Flt Lt Alward Scott RCAF caught fire after being hit by 20 mm AA rounds. Both Scott and his navigator, Flg Off Eric Fisher, bailed out. The other Mosquito crew watched the latter land in a clearing, but last saw Scott suspended in a tree, struggling to free himself. Their crashed aircraft was burning furiously about 200 yards away. Scott, who had been seriously wounded in the arm by the AA rounds, died from blood loss. Fisher returned to the squadron three weeks later, evading capture thanks to the help of friendly Burmese villagers and Force 136.

On 17 April, No 47 Sqn's Mosquitos carried bombs for the first time when three aircraft joined with seven from No 82 Sqn and two from No 45 Sqn. All were armed with 500-lb 11-second delay bombs to attack a trapped IJA division near Mawchi. Unfortunately, Flt Lt Norman Butler and Flt Sgt Frank Robson from No 47 Sqn crashed in HR519 just after take-off from Kumbhirgram. Their bombs exploded and the aircraft caught fire, killing the crew. The 11 remaining Mosquitos successfully attacked the enemy troop concentration, claiming direct hits on a powerhouse and buildings containing stores.

Groundcrew from No 110 Sqn service the starboard Merlin engine of HR629/VE-W at Joari. This aircraft was lost on 18 April 1945 whilst being flown by Flt Lt Raymond Rootes, with navigator Plt Off Stephen Blower, on an intruder mission along the Twante Canal in search of camouflaged motor torpedo boats (*Author's Collection*)

At Joari, after a stand-down on 9 April, No 110 Sqn continued to be tasked with attacking anything moving on roads, waterways and railways between Toungoo, Pegu and Moulmein. Mostly, crews operated in pairs, gaining operational experience.

On the 18th, two crews were tasked with searching the Twante Canal near Kawetkin for heavily camouflaged motor torpedo boats. Mosquito HR629, flown by Flt Lt Raymond Rootes, with navigator Plt Off Stephen Blower, failed to return. That same day, in preparation for the final assault on Rangoon, the commanders of both Nos 45 and 82 Sqns were advised of a move from Kumbhirgram to Joari. Two days later, Wg Cdr Duclos flew to Joari to make arrangements. There would be little let up in operations for both Nos 45 and 82 Sqns at Kumbhirgram, even whilst packing for Joari. Both units were managing six or more operational sorties per day, with new aircrew arriving as more tour-expired Australians departed for home.

Preparations to triple the number of Mosquitos operating from Joari were disrupted on 21 April when it was hit by a 'terrific downpour of rain', flooding aircrew tents, with many collapsing. The runway was rendered unserviceable for 48 hours. The next day, in Rangoon, Gen Heitaro Kimura, commander in chief of the Burma Area Army, ordered the IJA to covertly start leaving the city, with his own HQ making their way towards Moulmein, covered by a defensive rearguard action at Pegu.

On 24 April, No 110 Sqn launched 11 of its 12 serviceable Mosquitos in two operations against heavily camouflaged motor torpedo boats in Thonga. That same day, the first No 45 Sqn Mosquito arrived at Joari, followed by 100 groundcrew in Dakotas on the 26th. Having flown their final operations from Kumbhirgram on 27 April, 11 more Mosquitos from the unit were flown to Joari, together with 14 from No 82 Sqn.

There were doubts that Joari's runway would cope with three Mosquito squadrons, especially if it was hit by another downpour. The domestic arrangements were very rudimentary, with many having to make their own beds from bamboo. Food for the new arrivals was provided by No 110 Sqn until their messes were established, with Nos 82 and 45 Sqns deciding to operate a communal officers' mess. Before they had settled in, No 45 Sqn and the servicing echelon were notified that on 15 May they would be withdrawn from operations and rested at Chakulia.

The IJA, their prisoners and the Burmese locals were fully aware that the Allies were approaching Rangoon. Flt Sgt Johnny Yanota, a Mosquito navigator being held as a PoW in the city, recalled, 'Rumours started circulating as to how close our troops were, and air activity increased considerably'.

On 27 April, Nos 45 and 82 Sqns were still not operational at Joari. However, No 110 Sqn launched ten aircraft on four different night missions, one of which was a reconnaissance by a Mosquito pair of the Bay of Martaban. One of the aircraft (HR637) failed to return, with Flg Off St John Hawkins and Flt Sgt Wilfred Louis Allen being posted 'Missing, believed killed'.

By late April, the Mosquito conversion for No 47 Sqn at Kumbhirgam was at last complete. With the Fourteenth Army pressing southwards,

Formerly occupied by the IJAAF, Kinmagan airfield, 55 miles southwest of Mandalay, had a 6000-ft north–south uneven dirt runway and anti-blast shelters for dispersed aircraft. Most other facilities were primitive, however, with air- and groundcrew having to rely on basic tented accommodation. No 47 Sqn called the airfield home from 28 April to 15 August 1945. Resupplying Kinmagan would prove to be problematic, for it was nearly 400 miles away from the closest railhead and established servicing facilities in Assam *(SWWEC – LEEWW.2008.085 Bailey, D A)*

intruders were needed in central Burma to help prevent the IJA from regrouping at Moulmein or retreating into Thailand. On the 26th, after completing an evening 'rhubarb' along the Sittang River and railway lines northeast of Rangoon, two No 47 Sqn Mosquitos landed at Kinmagan, which would be the unit's new base.

Recently abandoned by the IJAAF, Kinmagan airfield was 55 miles southwest of Mandalay. Whilst it had a 6000-ft north–south uneven dirt runway and anti-blast shelters for dispersed aircraft, most other facilities were primitive, relying on basic tented accommodation. Drainage would clearly be a problem. Supplies would also be an issue because Kinmagan was nearly 400 miles from the closest Allied railhead and the Mosquito servicing facilities in Assam. Everything, including fuel, armaments, spare parts and food, required to keep the Mosquitos operational would need to be air-lifted to them.

The next day, Wg Cdr Filson-Young and a further eight Mosquitos relocated to Kinmagan. Within 24 hours they were operational, sending four pairs against different targets, strafing and bombing. On landing from his sortie, Plt Off Henry Milne suffered brake failure in RF658. Overshooting the runway, his Mosquito was written off.

On 29 April, as IV Corps advanced towards Rangoon in preparation for Operation *Dracula*, Operation *Freeborn* was launched. Luckily, the early monsoon weather did not hinder 28 transports airlifting a battalion from the 9th Indian Infantry Brigade to Pyuntaza airfield, 40 miles north of Rangoon and just north of Pegu, to cut off the IJA's escape route eastwards. The troops quickly cleared Pegu of the enemy, liberating 400 British and American PoWs being marched by the Japanese towards the Sittang River and Thailand in the process.

Operation *Dracula* would soon start, with paratroopers neutralising seaward-facing heavy guns, then a seaborne invasion with units of XV Corps entering the city from the Rangoon River estuary. Throughout, there would be extensive air support, including saturation bombing of strategic supply dumps by USAAF B-29 Superfortresses.

Sometimes the weather made flying impossible. On 30 April, No 82 Sqn's Flg Off Maude flew as Flg Off Wambeek's navigator;

'We were briefed for a rhubarb on the Rangoon River and, after taking off from Joari, we encountered massive cumulonimbus [clouds] in the Bay of Bengal. We couldn't get under them or round them and finally had to admit defeat and return to Joari.'

That same day, No 47 Sqn flew eight Mosquito sorties. Wg Cdr Filson-Young led four aircraft against a reported IJA concentration at Nammekon. Although the bashas that they bombed and strafed seemed deserted, the squadron's ORB noted that 'a report [was] later received from No 221 Group that many Jap casualties were caused and a stores dump set on fire'.

Rangoon jail was the main PoW camp in Burma, and in this 1 May 1945 photograph taken from a low-flying Mosquito, its different wings are clearly visible – as is the *JAPS GONE* message painted on the roof by prisoners as soon as the IJA guards had fled (*Tom Yanota Collection*)

Twenty-four hours earlier, in Rangoon jail, news of a fully loaded truck leaving the complex quickly spread, as did the lack of guards on the compound gates. Flt Sgt Yanota recalled that they shouted for a guard, and 'when none appeared, we yelled across to the Chinese compound and asked a prisoner named Anthony if he could see any guards. When he replied in the negative, Wg Cdr [William] Hudson [formerly CO of No 82 Sqn], acting as our CO in place of the more-senior Wg Cdr Hill, who was ill with dysentery, climbed over the fence to inform No 6 Compound of the state of affairs. He went over to their gate and started chatting with the English prisoners, and suddenly Flt Lt MacDonald noticed a note attached to the railings of the gate'. Dated that day, it confirmed that the 'Nipponese Army' had indeed left, and that the gate's keys were in the gate room.

The PoWs forced open the compound gate and did a quick reconnaissance of the camp. There were no IJA soldiers to be seen, so Yanota and other prisoners stood guard at the main gate to prevent local Burmese militia from entering the prison. Then they found a second note, attached to the main prison gate. This one was from Capt Haruo Ito, the prison commandant, stating that the PoWs were free, and that they could eat the food in the compound. It concluded with his hope to meet them all again 'on the battlefield'. With no guards to stop them, the PoWs released everyone in solitary confinement and painted *JAPS GONE* on the prison roof.

MAY 1945

On 1 May, the first phase of Operation *Dracula* was initiated. That night, 38 USAAF transports lifted off from Akyab carrying Gurkha paratroopers, successfully dropping them near the mouth of the Rangoon River. The Gurkhas met little resistance from the IJA rearguard.

Sgt Gordon Thewlis, a navigator with No 82 Sqn, recalled his 26th operation flown on 2 May;

'The task of 82 Squadron was to neutralise the gun positions, both ground artillery and anti-aircraft protecting an oil refinery situated at Syriam, about five miles to the south of Rangoon. It was essential to put these guns out of commission. Royal Marine Commandos were coming up the estuary in landing craft, and they would have been sitting ducks if the guns had still been operational. We were in two flights of four Mosquitos, each armed with two 500-lb bombs fitted with 11-second delay fuses.'

With Allied air activity now close by, PoWs like Sgt Yanota were worried;

'At 0930 hrs a Mosquito of 110 Squadron overshot its run on an unoccupied gun post just outside of our prison and its bomb hit the outer wall of the prison's eastern perimeter, just beyond No 6 Compound. Luckily, no one was hurt, but had that pilot been another

Wg Cdr Arthur 'Soapy' Saunders was the CO of No 110 Sqn, although this photograph of him was taken when he led No 418 Sqn RCAF in Britain prior to his posting to the Far East. On 2 May 1945, seeing *JAPS GONE* and *EXTRACT DIGIT* painted on the roof of Rangoon jail, Saunders landed his Mosquito at Mingaladon airfield and made his way into Rangoon to the jail. Having effectively 'liberated' the PoWs, he went on to prevent significant loss of life by notifying the troops leading Operation *Dracula* that the IJA had left Rangoon. Saunders perished on 11 July 1945 when Expeditor II HB158 in which he was being flown from Baigachi to Kinmagan failed to arrive at Feni (*RCAF PL7839*)

fraction of a second delayed in releasing his bomb, half of the jail's occupants would have been maimed and killed. We couldn't figure this close bombing out, so, in anger, but also with genuine concern for our welfare, we painted another rooftop message, *EXTRACT DIGIT*. Its meaning – "get your finger out" – could not possibly be mistaken as a Japanese ploy.'

Plt Offs Willis and Thompson of No 47 Sqn were tasked with their first operation from Kinmagan on 2 May, flying HR518 with five other Mosquitos. According to Willis;

'Huge thunderstorms, with storm clouds rising well over 25,000 ft, built up in the afternoon and then the heavens opened. This monsoon weather forced our return to base, with both the primary and secondary targets impossible to reach. Immediately upon landing, we enlarged the ditches around the tent that we had previously moved to a gently sloping site so as to give us better drainage. The rain came down in torrents, tent floors were awash and the open latrines overflowed.'

In the early afternoon, a No 110 Sqn Mosquito with unit CO, Wg Cdr Saunders, at the controls flew low over the centre of Rangoon. He had decided that he needed to verify what was painted on the roof of the city jail. Seeing the words *JAPS GONE* and *EXTRACT DIGIT*, he knew that he had to investigate further. His radio transmitter was faulty, but Saunders decided to land at the nearest former IJAAF airfield, Mingaladon. He and his navigator, Flt Lt James Stephen, hitched a lift into Rangoon and made for the jail, where they were greeted by Wg Cdr Hudson.

That evening Saunders set off with Stephen to halt Operation *Dracula* by commandeering a boat and heading up the Rangoon River towards the invasion force. Under the cover of darkness, a flotilla of ships had approached the coast and offloaded the 26th Indian Infantry Division in landing craft that were heading for Rangoon. The liberation of the city was underway. Against the odds, Saunders and Stephen met up with them, and by dawn the following morning (3 May) had persuaded the troops that they did not need to use force to take Rangoon.

Praying that Operation *Dracula* had indeed been postponed, early on the 3rd, Hudson sent Plt Off Emeny and two other RAF PoWs to Mingaladon with orders to make it safe so that Dakotas could land and evacuate their fellow prisoners. Meanwhile, at Joari, WO Murkin and Flt Sgt Carruthers of No 82 Sqn had taken off at 0800 hrs in their FB VI. In the early hours of 3 May, they had been tasked to support Operation *Dracula* by 'rhubarbing' south of Rangoon. Carruthers recalled, 'We were issued with a detailed map of Rangoon and its surrounds, delineating the area of each particular "rhubarb" that day'. They we recalled before attacking.

Meanwhile, the liberated PoWs still did not know what was happening, as Yanota explained;

'At 1430 hrs an RAF Liberator approached at low-level with its bomb-bay doors open and showered us with what we initially feared were 1000-lb bombs. At about 50 ft from the ground, however, parachutes opened to gently deposit numerous containers within the prison walls. The Liberator then circled around taking photos of the prison. Over the next 20 minutes, two more RAF Liberators made similar parcel-dropping runs. We were thrilled to receive 22 containers in total filled with delicious K-rations and much-needed medical stores.'

Within two days, the first PoWs were being evacuated from Mingaladon. With Rangoon liberated, the focus now was on completing the rout of the Japanese from Burma, Thailand and Southeast Asia.

No 47 Sqn was now capable of making a serious contribution to the prosecution of the air war in-theatre. On 2 May, 12 of its Mosquitos had undertaken a 'cab rank' mission over the Rangoon River for local ground controllers, who called individual aircraft down to 'bomb and strafe' Japanese positions. These operations continued for some days, although the high sortie tempo proved challenging for groundcrews tasked with maintaining No 47 Sqn's Mosquitos using the sparse facilities at Kinmagan, where temperatures were frequently in excess of 30°C. As Aircraftman Sandy Osterfield explained, just rearming was a challenge;

'Around the strip there was little cover to protect bombs, rocket heads and fuses from the hot sun. How do you cope when they are too hot to handle? We often parked the bombs under the aircraft wings, as they provided the best shelter.'

The operational tasking was similar for the three other intruder units, as No 82 Sqn's Sgt Thewlis explained. Joari allowed 'us to fly due south over the coast, then on a due east course to the Irrawaddy estuary, then northeast to Rangoon. This route meant we missed the highly dangerous monsoon clouds building up further inland in Burma'. However, extensive thunderstorms still affected operations. Flt Lt C L 'Twitch' Turner recalled;

'It was always piddling down with rain. It was very uncomfortable, particularly when one hit a monsoon cloud, which was diabolical – I hit one once and found myself upside down.'

Even with the IJA in retreat, aircraft were still lost. On 4 May, No 110 Sqn's RF586, flown by Flt Sgt Sid Hemingway, with navigator WO Phil Turner, failed to return.

No 45 Sqn was thwarted by the weather on both 3 and 4 May, with its aircraft being forced to return to base. The unit operated successfully over the next two days, but then, together with Nos 82 and 110 Sqns, moved to Chiringa because it had an all-weather strip – heavy rain was forecast. This meant that Chiringa became very crowded due to it now hosting six operational squadrons. Nevertheless, on 7 May, No 45 Sqn managed to complete two operations each of four aircraft from there, with crews successfully bombing, strafing and 'rhubarbing'.

There was little celebration amongst Mosquito crews on 8 May 1945 for Victory in Europe Day, since their war against Japan was not over. The operational pace continued at Chiringa – 'cab ranks', aircraft bombing and strafing bridges and troop concentrations, and 'rhubarbs' – through to the expected 'resting' of Nos 45 and 82 Sqns. On 12 May, having completed 1263 intruder sorties, No 45 Sqn was indeed rested.

That same day, No 82 Sqn flew its final two operations of the war. After 879 intruder sorties, Wg Cdr Snell was told that he and his aircrew were to remain on standby until the squadron was rested.

Flg Off Gordon 'Tiny' Lauder was killed in a flying accident shortly after No 45 Sqn stopped operations when the Harvard IIB that he was a passenger in crashed near Kumbhirgram when Flg Off Freddie Fortune lost control of the aircraft whilst flying inverted at low-level over Monierkhal Tea Estate in Paianghat – a place where they had spent two weeks on leave during March. In a letter written to Lauder's mother shortly after his death, Olive Smith, the plantation owner's wife, wrote, 'Both boys were killed instantaneously – they couldn't have known a thing about it.' (*Penny Hunt Collection*)

No 221 Group ordered No 110 Sqn to join No 47 Sqn at Kinmagan, which meant the unit also flew its last operations from the coastal sites on 12 May. The squadron's new challenge was to move its support equipment and supplies by road to Cox's Bazar now that the rainy season had begun. This took longer than expected, especially with No 110 Sqn personnel now finding themselves split between three locations – ten days would pass before the unit was fully operational at Kinmagan. On the night of 12 May, Chiringa was hit by a destructive storm, and when dawn broke the following day, it was clear that most of the domestic bashas had been badly damaged and some totally destroyed.

Tragically, even though No 45 Sqn had stopped operational flying, Flg Offs Freddie Fortune and Gordon 'Tiny' Lauder were killed in a flying accident in the unit's Harvard IIB FE614 on 14 May near Kumbhirgram. Fortune lost control of the aircraft during a low-level inverted flypast over Monierkhal Tea Estate in Paianghat.

The following day, eight No 47 Sqn crews were tasked with attacking a supply point and river crossing at Lagunbyo – a key location in an IJA escape route from the Sittang River valley south towards Thaton, Moulmein and, thence, Malaya. They flew as two formations of four aircraft, led in RF700 by Wg Cdr Filson-Young. The CO's regular navigator, Flt Lt McGlory, had just completed his tour, so Filson-Young, who was also effectively 'tour expired', was navigated by Flg Off Roger Waters.

WO Bill Powell, with his navigator, Sgt Maurice Jones, flew as the CO's No 2, the former recalling;

'The weather was reasonable, and we found the target without much difficulty. Lagunbyo was situated in a valley, and each of us was to drop our two 500 pounders in a dive-bombing attack. The CO waved to me in the No 2 position and then peeled off to the left, diving onto the target area at an angle of 45 degrees. I followed suit and, as I looked down halfway through my diving turn, saw to my horror the CO's aircraft crash and explode in a colossal fireball.

'I must have been in something of a daze as I made my attack, dropping both bombs in the target area and then carrying out a strafing run with cannon on the buildings which came into the gunsight as I pulled out of the dive. Only then was I able to switch on the intercom and let the other two crews in the first flight and the leader of the second flight, which was now close to the target, know what had happened.'

The cause of RF700's crash was unclear, Powell stating;

'The obvious conclusion was that the CO's aircraft had been shot up as he dived towards the target area, giving him and his navigator no chance to bail out.'

Despite being only 25 years old, the highly decorated Wg Cdr 'Billy' Filson-Young had completed 232 operational sorties prior to his death.

After ten days of uncertainty, it was finally decided that both Nos 45 and 82 Sqns would relocate to Cholavaram, near Madras, to prepare for the invasion of Malaya. They started packing up on 17 May. Some groundcrew were able to fly from Kumbhirgram to Cholavaram, but most had to take a long, tedious rail journey, finally arriving after ten days on 31 May.

With the loss of Wg Cdr Filson-Young and No 45 Sqn being rested, Wg Cdr Duclos was transferred from the latter unit to take command of

No 47 Sqn. Flt Lt H A Aykroyd, No 45 Sqn's senior flight commander, was promoted to take over this unit. The leadership of No 110 Sqn also changed. Having 'liberated Rangoon', Wg Cdr Saunders and navigator Flt Lt Stephen were transferred to duties with No 221 Group. On 17 May, No 110 Sqn was ordered to relocate to Kinmagan, where its senior flight commander, Sqn Ldr Peter Joel, was made CO with promotion to wing commander.

Despite all these command changes, intruding operations from Kingmagan continued unabated, with No 47 Sqn despatching three Mosquito pairs at different times to bomb and strafe on 17 May. The next day, it launched two Mosquito pairs and a single four-aircraft formation. The first pair aborted their attack and the second pair bombed and strafed a ferry near Duyinzeik. Finally, in the late afternoon, four Mosquitos were despatched to 'bomb and strafe 500 Japs harbouring in Anyapwa and Yantahya'. Their bombs were on target.

After ten days of being non-operational, No 110 Sqn Mosquitos flew into Kinmagan on 22 May to coincide with the arrival of their support staff and equipment. Two pairs were immediately in action that afternoon, 'rhubarbing' from Toungoo to Kanmamaung. They attacked a few vehicles and ten bashas.

The next sorties for No 110 Sqn came on 24 May when, according to the squadron ORB, having bombed and strafed Kyuaktan, near Yinyon, Capt Montgomery of the South African Air Force and his wingman, Flt Lt Brown, saw 'a column of Japs (100–150) marching in threes. They immediately dived into 20 yards of scrub on roadside'. Montgomery made four runs and Brown made three, with 'the whole [area] plastered by cannon fire – believed many casualties'. On 26 May, No 82 Sqn entrained at Chiringa and Kumbhirgram for their long, slow journey to Cholavaram.

JUNE 1945

It was hot and humid at Kinmagan as aircrew from Nos 47 and 110 Sqns acclimatised to their 'bomb and strafe' tasking. They were frequently directed by ground controllers manning Visual Control Posts, who would pass on timely intelligence such as '100 Japs dug in on hilltop' or 'Concentration of 700 Japs with MG [machine gun] at Mingon'. They managed to launch up to eight aircraft each day on these close support missions.

On 1 June, No 110 Sqn despatched four aircraft to attack targets in Natkyi. During the attack, RF589's starboard engine and VHF radio were hit by machine gun fire at 1002 hrs. Flt Lt Turner, leading the operation, accompanied the damaged aircraft to Mingaladon, where the pilot, Flt Lt Alan John, attempted an emergency landing at 1020 hrs. The Mosquito crashed, however, killing John and seriously injuring the navigator, Sgt Norman Keighley. Turner landed a few minutes later and, after attending to formalities, returned to Kinmagan that afternoon.

On 2 June, four Mosquitos from No 47 Sqn and two from No 110 Sqn attacked gun positions at Pauggyi and then strafed camp areas north of Moulmein. The monsoon was never far away at this time, as No 47 Sqn's Plt Off Willis recalled;

'Flying often involved going through heavy rain, with the reduced visibility making it far from easy in trying to judge the way forward through towering masses of cloud. The windscreen wiper worked overtime.'

On 5 June, four No 47 Sqn Mosquitos attacked 500 IJA troops near a wireless station at Nyaungbo. Willis, flying RF713, was very satisfied with the outcome;

'Our aircraft fired 450 20 mm shells and 1000 rounds of .303 machine gun bullets. As with other occasions, a later report indicated we had very effectively dispersed the Japanese troop concentration, inflicting many casualties.'

The following day, No 110 Sqn despatched four aircraft on an early morning 'bomb and strafe' raid on an IJA headquarters at Kunzeik. Although the cloud base en route was at just 500 ft, the pilots dropped 16 500-lb 11-second delay bombs on target. They then completed 20 strafing runs which 'resulted in many Japs being killed'.

On 7 June, the monsoon hit hard, with heavy rain closing Kinmagan's airstrip for seven days.

On 13 June, Flt Lt Geoffrey Tonks and Flt Sgt Geoffrey Cook, newly arrived on No 45 Sqn in Cholavaram, were killed during training when Mosquito HR372 hit high-tension wires across a ravine. The following day, with the ground finally drying out, No 47 Sqn managed to launch two operational sorties from Kinmagan. On 15 June, the weather was not good enough for operations, but both squadrons managed to get 12 Mosquitos airborne to participate in Mountbatten's victory parade in Rangoon. Most other invited aircraft did not make it, apart from some Spitfires based near Rangoon.

The weather was also good enough for Wg Cdr Duclos to be flown into Kinmagan from Cholavaram to take command of No 47 Sqn on 17 June. Sadly, later that same day, having survived 60 operations with No 45 Sqn, Flg Off Ron Wilcock, who had flown Duclos by Mosquito from Cholavaram, failed to make it back to base – in HR309 – and was posted 'Missing, believed killed', along with his passenger, Flg Off Leonard Soulsby of Thunderbolt II-equipped No 34 Sqn (which was also based at Kinmagan). Several replacement crews from Britain also reached No 47 Sqn on the 17th before the airstrip was closed again for 24 hours.

Over the next few days, the two Kinmagan-based squadrons despatched nearly 40 Mosquitos on 'bomb and strafe' operations to multiple targets. Sqn Ldr Ira Sutherland RNZAF, one of No 110 Sqn's flight commanders, led five Mosquitos in an attack on enemy troops concentrated around a sawmill in Nutka. Between them they dropped 14 500-lb bombs, 12 of which were on target, and completed 23 strafing runs from all directions.

Wg Cdr Duclos led his first No 47 Sqn operation on 20 June, which saw four FB VIs sent out to 'bomb and strafe'. With the cloud base at 200 ft over their primary target, the crews diverted to their alternative – a transit camp under construction. Eleven of their 12 bombs landed on target in the bashas, and after strafing, they returned to base.

Poor weather conditions continued to blight the area. Completing a successful operation on 21 June, Flg Offs Alan Saunders and John Wise of No 47 Sqn experienced starboard undercarriage failure in RF757 upon landing back at Kinmagan. Although the aircraft was damaged enough to be declared a write-off, both crewmen were unhurt in the incident. On 25 June, six aircraft from No 47 Sqn successfully damaged a bypass bridge, as well as dropping six- and 12-hour delay bombs to hinder rebuilding. Then, during a 'rhubarb' on the Moulmein railway that same day, WO Ken

Illingworth and Flt Sgt George Tuck crashed in RF716 whilst following another Mosquito in an attack on a 'three-tonner' (truck). Their aircraft was seen 'burning on the ground'.

Meanwhile, No 110 Sqn increased its daily sortie rate. On 21 June, despite 'cloud on the deck, heavy rain', six crews still managed to 'bomb and strafe' their targets in the Duyinzeik area. The next day, Sqn Ldr Sutherland led eight Mosquitos against a concentration of IJA troops. On the 23rd, two flights of four aircraft were again despatched to Duyinzeik, contending with very poor weather over the target. Nine Mosquitos were sortied on 26 June, when the weather at the three targets was reported, respectively, as '8/10 s/cumulus base 300ft', 'clouds on hill tops but clear in valleys' and '8/10 s/cumulus on deck, visibility 500ft to nil'. The attack on the third target was aborted.

A52-526/NA-E of No 1 Sqn RAAF was one of two camouflaged Mosquitos (the other being A52-505/NA-Q) from the unit to stage through Morotai on 18 March 1945 on their way to Manila, in the Philippines, for testing against captured Japanese aircraft. In transit, the Mosquito's crew (pilot Flg Off Alex Barras and navigator Plt Off Eric Hart) strafed a barge and huts in New Guinea to thus become the first RAAF Mosquito to fire its guns in anger. Eventually repainted silver, A52-526 subsequently flew with No 1 Sqn from Labuan (*Philip Jarrett Collection*)

On 27 June, Wg Cdr Joel led seven aircraft on a bridge attack ('10/10 stratus, base 500/700ft heavy rain'), whilst two aircraft completed an offensive reconnaissance on the Moulmein railway. That afternoon, with his departure for his posting to Britain imminent, Sutherland flew alone in Mosquito RF582 to Akyab to bid farewell to friends. The next morning, he took off at 1150 hrs to return to Kinmagan but was never seen again. Eventually, wreckage was found which showed that Sutherland's aircraft had probably disintegrated in mid-air – RF582 had previously been withdrawn from operational flying because of its poor condition.

Having converted from the Beaufort to the Mosquito FB VI in Kingaroy, Queensland, in January 1945, the RAAF's No 1 Sqn had finally been deployed to Morotai, in what was then the Netherlands East Indies' Malaku Islands, in May. Through June, it had supported Australian forces in the battle to regain Labuan, an island off Borneo. The unit only flew a few missions against the Japanese, its deployment to Labuan being delayed by the need to extend the island's runway so that the Mosquito could operate. One aircraft was lost in action.

For the final few days of June 1945, weather permitting, No 110 Sqn continued to attack fuel and ammunition dumps, whilst No 47 Sqn focused on IJA troop concentrations.

JULY 1945

The 'bombing and strafing' operations now focused on large groups of troops from the IJA's 28th Army that were hiding in the ravines of the Pegu Yoma, intent on crossing the Sittang River to escape to Thailand. On 3 July, the IJA's 33rd Army came to their aid by trying to secure Sittang Bend. However, British forces, having captured the enemy's breakout plans, blocked troop movements and attacked with artillery, Spitfires and Thunderbolts. The 33rd finally withdrew after four days of pummelling from both the ground and the air, although the Allies knew that it would try again.

Three pristine Mosquito FB VIs of No 1 Sqn are put through their paces during a patrol from Labuan in mid-1945. A52-500, closest to the camera, was destroyed on 11 August 1945 during an aborted take-off from Labuan, the Mosquito skidding sideways and running off the airstrip into mud. The aircraft in the middle of the formation is A52-526, now repainted (*Public Domain*)

Early on the 3rd, No 110 Sqn launched six aircraft against 'four Jap-held villages in Kyauktaung area'. Unfortunately, RF600 hit a bump during take-off, bounced and a wing hit the ground. Plt Off Hendrick Van der Pol could not prevent the aircraft from crashing, and both he and Flt Sgt James Gordon were killed. The remaining five aircraft bombed on target and then strafed, although they subsequently noted that strafing runs were 'difficult due to the nature of the terrain'.

Over the next six days, No 110 Sqn completed 39 intruder sorties in ten operations. On 8–9 July the unit was directly involved in the Battle of the Sittang Bend, and on the 10th Wg Cdr Joel noted, 'It is becoming increasing evident that our aircraft are being overworked, and serviceability is suffering. We are reduced to eight available aircraft'. No 47 Sqn despatched 34 aircraft on eight operations over the same period, primarily bombing and strafing enemy troop concentrations in support of the Army.

On 12 July, No 110 Sqn despatched three Mosquitos to bomb 'a Jap ration dump' in the centre of Shwehle. Unfortunately, RF672 crashed into paddy fields 800 yards north of the target, the aircraft disintegrating. Flg Off Leo O'Neill and Flt Lt David Cookson were killed on impact with the ground.

Three days later, the IJA's 28th Army attempted to break out from the Pegu Yoma, still unaware that its plans were in British hands. The Japanese troops would be forced to run the gauntlet of two specially created 'killing fields' on either side of the main highway that had been chosen as a key escape route. The first 'field' was for artillery and the second was for ground attack aircraft. Burmese guerrillas helped coordinate air attacks from the east bank of the Sittang River, ambushing escaping IJA forces and 'cutting them to pieces'. It was highly effective, as one of the guerrilla leaders reported;

'You are killing hundreds of Japs, and your perfect coordination and patience in reading our crude signals is saving the lives of many thousands of defenceless civilians.'

The battle, a bloodbath for the IJA, lasted for days.

On 17 July, four No 110 Sqn Mosquitos were tasked with 'bombing and strafing' the railway at Apalon. During the attack, RF705 was damaged by a bomb that had possibly exploded instantaneously upon release. With the aircraft's main fuel tanks holed, Flg Off Charles Locke, with WO Donald Nicolson, immediately headed for Rangoon. Locke eventually ditched in shallow water on mudflats, breaking RF705's back. Although he was picked up by an Air Sea Rescue boat, no trace was ever found of Nicolson, who was posted 'Missing, believed killed'.

For the next week both Nos 47 and 110 Sqns continued 'bombing and strafing' IJA troop concentrations, providing ground support, with many of the sorties being part of the extended Battle of the Sittang Bend. Sometimes the weather prevented crews from reaching their primary targets, and often their bombing runs were flown at 50–80 ft due to the low cloud base.

Winston Churchill resigned as Prime Minister on 26 July after a humiliating electoral defeat to Labour's Clement Atlee. That same day, the Allies issued the Potsdam Declaration calling for unconditional Japanese surrender. If this was not accepted, they warned that there would be 'prompt and utter destruction'. Ten days previously, the Manhattan Project, developing the atomic bomb, had successfully completed its live Trinity Test with a plutonium implosion device in New Mexico. The Americans now committed to preparing the Little Boy and Fat Man bombs to bring an end to the conflict.

It did not come as a surprise to Allied High Command when Japan rejected the Potsdam Declaration on 29 July. Although the Allies continued with their plans to defeat the enemy, for the Mosquito squadrons, fewer and fewer aircraft were now serviceable and the delivery of replacements had virtually stopped.

On 31 July, No 47 Sqn's Flg Off Reg Davis, with Flt Sgt Bert Reich, in HR500; Flt Lt Powell, with Flg Off Busby, in RF695; and WOs Byatt and Horn in HR523 were briefed for a 'bomb and strafe' operation. Armed with four 500-lb 11-second delay bombs each, the crews were forced to divert to their secondary target – a hospital area in Moulmein that the IJA was using as a barracks – due to thunderstorms. The Mosquitos attacked at roof-top height at 280 mph, bombing simultaneously in sticks of four. The AA fire was concentrated, but after the bombing run they attacked a ship and bashas, before departing for home. A Force 136 report dated 2 August 1945 stated that 'nine direct hits and two near misses were scored on the buildings and one direct hit on a flak position. Over 400 bodies were recovered from the debris'.

AUGUST 1945

On the first two days of August, No 47 Sqn sortied six aircraft on 'bomb and strafe' operations against troop concentrations, whilst No 110 Sqn managed to despatch 16 Mosquitos on similar raids. Heavy rain then rendered the dispersals unserviceable for three days.

On the 6th, the USAAF dropped the Little Boy atomic bomb on Hiroshima, with devastating effect. Japan did not immediately capitulate, however. By then, Nos 47 and 110 Sqns could now get their aircraft from the dispersals to the airstrip, allowing some Mosquito operations to resume. On 9 August, the Americans increased the pressure on Japan by dropping the Fat Man atomic bomb on Nagasaki. Again, the impact was devastating, both weapons delivered 'prompt and utter destruction' as had been promised on 26 July. In respect to the use of the bombs No 110 Sqn's ORB noted;

'There has been a great deal of discussion on the subject of the new atomic bomb, and general opinion seems to be a little fearful of the possibilities opened up by this discovery. However, it is felt that this, coupled with the entry of Russia in the war against Japan, is likely to cause capitulation at an early date.'

Air- and groundcrew from 'B' Flight of No 45 Sqn pose for a photograph with an FB VI on 15 August 1945 to celebrate VJ Day at Cholavaram (*James Payne, Through their Eyes*)

Waterlogged dispersals prevented operations on 10 August, allowing time for the squadrons to prepare for a move south to Hmawbi airfield.

In London, after another meeting to discuss Mosquito airframe failures, Vernon Brown, the Chief Inspector of Accidents, released its minutes, concluding, 'The susceptibility of the Mosquito to break up during a pull-out shows that, considering the manoeuvrability and stability characteristics, the aircraft is weak structurally. The high fatality rate may be attributed to the cramped accommodation and the extreme difficulty in leaving the cockpit once the aircraft structure has failed'. The team had investigated 69 Mosquito structural failures, but none of those that had plagued the squadrons in the Far East.

Operations over Burma had been winding down. Seven days after Nagasaki, on 15 August, Emperor Hirohito spoke for the first time on the radio to announce the unconditional surrender of Japan's armed forces. On the 16th, both Nos 47 and 110 Sqns started their relocation to Hmawbi, with the serviceable aircraft, their aircrew and some groundcrew flying there as the advance party. Everyone else followed by road, taking several days. Meanwhile, the aircrew and groundcrew advance party settled into their new tented accommodation.

Everyone was in a celebratory mood after the Japanese surrender. Having over-imbibed most of the day, recently promoted Sqn Ldr Turner, spent the evening relaxing with fellow officers. Taking an early 'rain check', he returned to his nearby tent to sleep. Then, their camp was subjected to a grenade attack by IJA troops who had not surrendered. Luckily, no one was killed, although two people suffered burst ear drums and others received shrapnel injuries. Flg Off Syd Parker, a No 47 Sqn pilot, was caught by a grenade blast and thrown into a monsoon ditch;

'Some hours later I was in a military hospital with both eardrums burst, a massive bruise from calf to shoulder and having bits of metal picked out of my back.'

The disapproving army medical officer called out of bed to treat the casualties initially believed that he was dealing with the effects of celebratory excesses at an RAF Mess.

Mosquito FB VI HP884 of No 47 Sqn sits at Hmawbi airfield sometime after the unit moved there from Kinmagan on 15 August 1945. This aircraft remained with the squadron until it was struck off charge on 28 February 1946, just three weeks before the unit disbanded at Butterworth, in Malaya (*Philip Jarrett Collection*)

The war was still not over. 'On 20 August 1945, out of the blue came an SOS for help from a section of our guerrilla Force 136 that was being attacked by Japs [at Tikedo] who would not accept surrender,' recalled Sqn Ldr Turner. 'I led the raid that put paid to this problem.' Under his command, eight No 110 Sqn Mosquitos took off in two groups of four between 1423–1438 hrs, heading for three separate targets near Tikedo. The first four attacked their target just after 1457 hrs and had returned to Hmawbi by 1554 hrs. A pair then bombed their target at 1517 hrs and landed back at base at 1604 hrs.

The final Mosquito pair were flown by Flt Lt Ron Prankerd, with Flg Off George Richards navigating, in RF731, and WO Alan Rendell, with navigator WO Bell, in HR562. Their target was bashas surrounded by trees at reference QG426815. HR562's undercarriage would not retract after take-off, so Rendell fell behind resolving the problem. Prankerd arrived over the target at 1510 hrs and loitered for more than ten minutes until Rendell arrived. Both aircraft completed their attacks at 1525 hrs, with Prankerd releasing bombs first, followed by Rendell. The two aircraft landed back at base at 1606 hrs.

For the RAF, World War 2 was now finally over. Turner added, 'It was established later that on this raid the last bomb of the war was dropped by the RAF – the pilot who actually dropped it was WO Rendell.' Purely by chance, this created some real symmetry in World War 2, since No 110 Sqn had dropped both the RAF's first and last bombs of the conflict – the first Allied offensive operation of the war was on 4 September 1939 when five No 110 Sqn Blenheim IVs were sent on a low-level bombing raid to the German port of Wilhemshaven.

On 22 August, the groundcrew convoys finally reached Hmawbi. Four days later, the Japanese surrender delegation arrived at the airfield. WOs Ray Hicks and Jack Goodwin of No 47 Sqn immediately flew the 'surrender documents' to HQ SEAC in Ceylon. Upon their arrival in the afternoon, no one wanted to take the papers so late in the day, so Hicks looked after them overnight and handed them in the following morning.

It was not until 2 September 1945, just one day short of six years since Britain declared war on Germany in 1939, that the official documents confirming the surrender of the Japanese forces were signed in Tokyo Bay. The war had been over for several months in Europe by then, allowing most of combatants from this theatre to return home. This further added to the feeling long held by those still in Burma that they were part of a 'forgotten war'.

Despite Japan's surrender, a number of RAF units remained in India. No 211 Sqn, for example, had only started converting to the Mosquito FB VI from the Beaufighter X at Yelahanka in June 1945 in preparation for the invasion of Malaya. Four squadron members lost their lives in training accidents. Having completed the conversion, the unit moved to St Thomas Mount, near Madras, in early November 1945. By month-end No 211 Sqn was based in Don Muang, Thailand, with a detachment in Akyab, Burma. It was eventually disbanded in March 1946. Nos 47, 82 and 110 Sqns also disbanded at around this time, leaving No 45 Sqn as the last Mosquito FB VI-equipped unit in-theatre – it would continue to fly the aircraft until June 1947.

APPENDICES

Strike/Intruder operational sorties by squadron						
Month	**No 27 Sqn**	**No 45 Sqn**	**No 82 Sqn**	**No 47 Sqn**	**No 110 Sqn**	**Total**
December 1943 – March 1944	45	-	-	-	-	45
September 1944	-	2	-	-	-	2
October 1944	-	108	-	-	-	108
November 1944	-	36	-	-	-	36
December 1944	-	159	27	-	-	186
January 1945	-	217	198	-	-	415
February 1945	-	171	182	14	-	367
March 1945	-	352	269	126	2	749
April 1945	-	136	135	91	131	493
May 1945	-	82	68	217	127	494
June–July 1945	-	-	-	217	126	343
August 1945	-	-	-	25	42	67
Total	**45**	**1263**	**879**	**690**	**428**	**3305**

Aircrew deaths by Strike/Intruder squadron in both operations and during training						
Month	**No 27 Sqn**	**No 45 Sqn**	**No 82 Sqn**	**No 47 Sqn**	**No 110 Sqn**	**Total**
December 1943 – March 1944	2	-	-	-	-	2
April–August 1944	-	1	-	-	-	1
September 1944	-	2	2	-	-	4
October 1944	-	2	2	-	-	4
November 1944	-	3	2	-	-	5
December 1944	-	2	2	-	-	4
January 1945	-	6	1	-	-	7
February 1945	-	5	2	-	-	7
March 1945	-	2	6	-	-	8
April 1945	-	-	-	2	6	8
May 1945	-	2	-	2	4	8
June–July 1945	-	3	-	2	9	14
August 1945	-	-	-	-	-	0
Total	**2**	**28**	**17**	**6**	**19**	**72**

COLOUR PLATES COMMENTARY

1
Mosquito F II DZ695 of No 27 Sqn, RAF Agartala, India, 11 April 1943

This aircraft was sent to India for weather trials and evaluation with No 27 Sqn. Having flown two operations, DZ695 suffered an engine failure and overran the end of Agartala's runway during an emergency single-engine landing on 3 May 1943, injuring both Flg Off Fielding and Sgt Steer. The aircraft was struck off charge as unrepairable.

2
Mosquito FB VI HJ811 of No 27 Sqn, RAF Allahabad, India, October 1943

The first FB VI to arrive in India, having suffered engine trouble three times en route, HJ811 was allocated initially to No 27 Sqn and flew some operations with the unit in early 1944 prior to being transferred to No 45 Sqn at RAF Yelahanka in April of that year. The aircraft was eventually stuck off charge on 1 May when, during a transit flight from Yelahanka to RAF Amarda Road, an engine cut out, resulting in an emergency landing at Rajalmundy, during which the aircraft was written off.

3
Mosquito FB VI HX821/K of No 27 Sqn, RAF Agartala, India, February 1944

After flying a few operations with No 27 Sqn, HX821 was transferred to No 45 Sqn in April 1944. Six months later, following use in conversion and operational training with the latter squadron, it was sent to No 143 RSU at Bishnapur for rectification after its pilot, Sqn Ldr Norman Bourke, had noticed the leading edge starting to buckle. Following repair, HX821 broke up in the air at 8000 ft during a test flight on 10 October, killing Flt Lt Richard 'Dick' Campbell and engineer Flt Lt Douglas William Rimmell. Subsequent investigation of the wreckage revealed blood and feathers at a point of impact where a kite hawk had broken the plywood skin near where the main spar failed at the scarf joint.

4
Mosquito PR IX LR445/F of No 684 Sqn, RAF Dum Dum, India, April 1944

On 10 April 1944 Flt Lt 'Koss' Newman and Flt Sgt Ray Smith flew a 2256-mile round trip from RAF Ramu to photograph Nancowry Harbour on the island of Great Nicobar, their target being at the limit of the PR IX's range. LR445 was eventually struck off charge on 5 July 1945.

5
Mosquito FB VI HP939/OB-A of No 45 Sqn, RAF Amarda Road, India, May 1944

Just five days into the No 9 Fighter Refresher Course at RAF Amarda Road, Wg Cdr Harley Stumm had just completed practising 'quarter attacks' against a USAAF B-25, capturing it on cine film, when, approaching the airfield at 200 mph at 3600 ft, he appeared to lose control of HP939 and it rolled and dived into a near vertical spin. Pieces of the aircraft broke off in mid-air before it crashed into the ground. Both Stumm, No 45 Sqn's CO, and his navigator, Flt Lt Walter McKerracher, were killed. HP939 was thought to be the first Mosquito to have suffered structural failure in India.

6
Mosquito FB VI HP867/OB-Z of No 45 Sqn, RAF Dalbumgarh, India, 24 June 1944

Three aircraft were on a low-level training exercise near Bishnapur when Plt Off Cliff Emeny, flying HP867, struck the branch of a tree, damaging the mainplane, tailplane and starboard engine. He belly-landed the Mosquito in a paddy field and it broke up on impact with paddy field walls. Emeny and WO John Yanota walked away from the crash with relatively minor injuries, although the former was hospitalised for about a week and had three weeks' convalescence.

7
Mosquito FB VI HP886/UX-H of No 82 Sqn, RAF Kolar, India, 13 September 1944

HP886 'crashed unaccountably' whilst carrying out high-g quarter turns and attacks on another aircraft at an altitude of 5000 ft near RAF Kolar. Flg Off William Tuffnel and Flt Sgt Victor Abel were both killed. Witnesses said that the Mosquito disappeared underneath the target aircraft, possibly being thrown upside down.

8
Mosquito PR XVI NS688 (subsequently assigned to No 684 Sqn), RAF Dum Dum, India, November 1944

Crewed by Flt Lt L Linton and WO E J Gouldie, NS688 landed at Karachi after a record-breaking transit flight from Britain in November 1944. It completed the journey, with stops at El Adem, in Libya, and Shaibah, in Iraq, in just 16 hr 45 min, beating the previous record by 5 hr 27 min. The Mosquito was painted with 'invasion stripes' and the word *SNAKE* on the rear fuselage, with both markings having been introduced on 1 May 1943 to identify aircraft specifically destined for India, and to deter the practice common amongst senior commanders and units in the Mediterranean region who frequently 'hijacked' them as they passed through. Both were removed soon after its arrival at Dum Dum. NS688 subsequently served with No 684 Sqn.

9
Mosquito FB VI HR374/OB-Z of No 45 Sqn, RAF Kumbhirgram, India, 9 November 1944

Plt Off Emeny and WO Yanota were flying HR374 on the latter's 17th operation when, during a low-level attack on Meiktila airfield, the aircraft lost one engine to AA fire. After suffering further damage during an attack from an 'Oscar', Emeny made a belly landing. Having both escaped from the aircraft as it started to burn, the crew was about four miles from the crash when they were captured. Emeny and Yanota duly became PoWs in Rangoon jail.

10
Mosquito PR XVI NS645/P of No 684 Sqn, RAF Alipore, India, late 1944

This aircraft remained in service until late 1945, by which time it had been given the aircraft letter 'A'. On 14 November 1945, 20 minutes after take-off from Tan Son Nhat airfield, Saigon, in French Indochina, on a photo-reconnaissance survey mission, one of NS645's Rolls-Royce Merlin 76-series engines cut due to a faulty glycol system. Flg Off Keith Rawcliffe headed back to Saigon, where he belly landed, destroying the aircraft. Both he and his navigator, WO Anthony Sams, were also injured.

11
Mosquito FB VI HR403/UX-B of No 82 Sqn, RAF Kumbhirgram, India, 19 December 1944

Wg Cdr Lionel 'Bill' Hudson, CO of No 82 Sqn, was determined to perform the unit's first intruder operation. With WO Jack Shortis as his navigator, Hudson was flying low above the Irrawaddy River when his propellers hit the surface of the water. HR403 subsequently crashed into the jungle, and although Hudson and Shortis survived, they became PoWs in Rangoon jail.

12
Mosquito FB VI HR402/OB-C of No 45 Sqn, RAF Kumbhirgram, India, 7 January 1945

HR402 was shot down by Ki-43s on 15 January 1945, crashing eight miles north of Thedaw. Flt Lt Charles Goodwin and Flg Off Samuel Potts were killed.

13
Mosquito FB VI HR567/OB-D of No 45 Sqn, RAF Kumbhirgram, India, 10 February 1945

Whilst taking part in Operation *Cloak* on 10 February 1945, HR567 suffered a complete electrical failure just as its ordnance was dropped by WO 'Benny' Walsh and Flt Sgt 'Ossie' Orsborn. Attempting to return to base, the crew became lost. They eventually found the recently re-captured airstrip at Onbauk and landed, damaging the Mosquito when it crashed into a wrecked Dakota. Walsh and Orsborn were unhurt and the aircraft was salvaged by a maintenance unit and repaired.

14
Mosquito FB VI HR567/OB-F of No 45 Sqn, RAF Kumbhirgram, India, 4 April 1945

HR567 is depicted here in artwork in the scheme it wore after it had been returned to No 45 Sqn following repairs and a repaint. Having bombed an IJA base at Zinga at dusk on 4 April, its crew of WO Walsh and Flt Sgt Orsborn found themselves having to guide HR332 back to base after the latter aircraft lost its airspeed indicator. Running low on fuel, Walsh attempted an emergency landing at Monywa, but ran out of runway and HR567 lost its undercarriage upon hitting an AA gun position. HR332, following close behind, then crashed into it. Walsh and Orsborn were unhurt, as were Flg Offs Freddie Fortune and Joe Mears in HR332. Both Mosquitos were struck off charge, however.

15
Mosquito FB VI RF700/KU-V of No 47 Sqn, RAF Kinmagan, Burma, 30 April 1945

No 47 Sqn CO Wg Cdr 'Billy' Filson-Young, who had already completed his operational tour, decided to fly one last mission – in RF700 – on 30 April 1945. This proved to be a fateful decision, for he and navigator Flg Off Roger Waters were killed when they flew into the ground whilst dive-bombing an IJA supply point and river crossing at Lagunbyo.

16
Mosquito FB VI RF582/VE-K of No 110 Sqn, RAF Joari, India, 2 May 1945

Wg Cdr Arthur Saunders, CO of No 110 Sqn, and Flt Lt James Stephen landed RF582 at Mingaladon, north of Rangoon, on 2 May 1945 and 'liberated' the PoWs at Rangoon jail. Six weeks later, on 28 June, RF582 broke up in the air, killing the aircraft's sole occupant, Sqn Ldr Ira Sutherland. RF582 had previously been withdrawn from operational flying because of its poor condition.

17
Mosquito FB VI HR551/UX-P of No 82 Sqn, RAF Joari, India, early May 1945

This aircraft's last operation took place on 8 May 1945 when WOs John McDonald and Blackburn flew it on a 'rhubarb' to strafe and bomb targets of opportunity along the Salween (now renamed Thanlyin) River up to Kamarmaung. Later that month, No 82 Sqn was transferred to Cholavaram and placed in reserve. HR551 was eventually struck off charge on 8 October 1946.

18
Mosquito PR 34 RG203/E of No 684 Sqn, Cocos Island, July 1945

Mosquito PR 34s, including this aircraft, of No 684 Sqn were able to photograph the Malay capital Kuala Lumpur on several occasions before the Japanese surrender.

19
Mosquito FB VI RF711/A of No 211 Sqn, RAF Yelahanka, India, early July 1945

No 211 Sqn did not see operational service with Mosquitos before the Japanese surrender. Depicted here armed with RP-3s fitted to underwing rocket projectile rails, RF711 was eventually struck off charge after it crashed at Don Muang (home to the unit from late November 1945) on 31 January 1946.

20
Mosquito PR XVI MM367/U of No 684 Sqn, RAF Alipore, India, July 1945

Unlike other photo-reconnaissance Mosquitos assigned to No 684 Sqn which were finished in blue, this aircraft was painted in silver dope and featured standard SEAC theatre recognition markings. MM367, which had previously been allocated the aircraft letter 'M', was eventually struck off charge on 25 July 1946.

21
Mosquito FB VI HR562/VE-T of No 110 Sqn, RAF Hmawbi, Burma, 20 August 1945

Due to a problem with its undercarriage retracting, HR562 was the last of four Mosquitos to drop bombs during an operation against former IJA forces near Tikedo on 20 August. This meant that the aircraft's crew, WOs Alan Rendell and Bell, dropped the last RAF bombs of World War 2.

22
Mosquito FB 40 A52-500/NA-A of No 1 Sqn RAAF, Labuan Island, August 1945

Built in Britain by Standard Motors as HR302, this aircraft relieved production problems with the Australian-built FB 40 by being shipped out to Australia as the first of a batch of 38 FB VIs which were used to re-equip No 1 Sqn. It was taken on strength by the RAAF as A52-500 and written off on 11 August 1945 when Flt Lt William Shaw (with Plt Off James Robinson as his navigator) lost control after aborting his third attempt to take off from the airfield on Labuan Island. The aircraft skidded sideways and went off the strip into mud.

INDEX

Page numbers in **bold** refer to illustrations, in brackets tc captions and in *italics* to tables.

Abel, Flt Sgt Victor 37, **37**, 94
Accident Investigation Branch (AIB), RAF 35–37, 41
accidents 31, 35–39, 41, 85, 91, 92
air squadrons
  No 27 Sqn 10, 26, 29–30
  No 45 Sqn 30–34, 40, 41, 42–44, 45, 57–60, 61–63, 64, 70, 73–74, 75, 76, 76–77, **78**, 80, 84, 85–86, **90**
  No 47 Sqn 62, 68, 69–70, 79, 80–81, 83, 84, 85–88, 89, 90, 91
  No 82 Sqn 41, 44–45, 57–58, 59, 60–61, 63–64, 67, 68, 70, 71, 73–74, 75, 82, 84
  No 110 Sqn 63, 73, 74, 78, 79–80, **79**, 83, 84–85, 86–87, 88, 89, 90, 91–92
  No 681 Sqn 18, 19, 20, 23
  No 684 Sqn 18–20, 21, 22, 23–24, 25
Andrews, Flt Lt Cliff **20**, 24–25, **25**

Ball, Flt Sgt Ted 26, 26–27, **28**
Blinch, WO 'Jackie' 26, 27, 28, **28**
bridges 29, 32, 43, 44, 64, 71, 72–73, **72**, 75
Burma-Siam railway 19, 21, 24

cameras **21**, 24
Campbell, Flt Lt Richard 'Dick' 16–17, 23–24, 37, **38**, **39**, 44, 94
Carruthers, Flt Sgt Charles 67–68, 83
casualties and losses 19, 20, 28, 31, **31**, 34, 57, 58, 61, 70, 75, 78, 79, 85, 89, *93*
Chabot, Sqn Ldr C J 38–39, 41
cockpits **13**

development and testing 6–11
  constructicn materials 7
  fuselage 7, **8**
  initial evaluation 10–11
  production 8–9
  structure/structural failures 35, 35–41, 44, 63, 91
  testing 7–8, 35–36
  wings **8**, 36, 39–40
distance records 23–25
Duclos, Flt Lt Victor 'Duke' 33, 34, 66, 75, 76, 79, 85–86, 87

Earthquake operations 64
Emeny, Plt Off Cliff 16, 28, 29, 42, 43, 83, 94
engines 13, 14–15, 16–17, 22–23
Ewing, Flg Off Peter **60**, 64

ferrying 12–17
Filson-Young, Wg Cdr William 'Billy' 73, 79, 81, 85

Garnham, Flg Off Rex **42**, **65**, 66
Gotch, Sqn Ldr Chris 60–61
groundings 35–41, 43
Gunn, Plt Off William 'Billy' 26–27, 28, **28**

Harper, Flt Lt Frank 72, 74–75
Havilland, Gecffrey de 6–7, **7**, 8, 9, 35–36, 39–40, 41
Havilland, Maj Hereward de 40–41
Hudson, Wg Cdr Lionel 'Bill' 44–45, 82, 83, 95

Irvine, Flt Lt Jack **18**, 24–25

Japan
  halting the Japanese advance 9–10
  surrender 91, 92
Jones, Sqn Ldr Basil 18, 21–22

Kinmagan airfield **80**, 81, 83, 84–85, 86–87

Lauder, Flg Off Gordon 'Tiny' **84**, 85

McLellan Flg Off Walter 'Wal' 31, 73–74
Mahoney, Flt Lt G F 63–64
markings and paint **35**, **48** (94), **58**, **68**, 76, **88**
Maude, Flg Off Arthur 38, 66, 71, 81
medals and awards
  Distinguished Service Order 75
  Victoria Cross 26
Mooney, WO Brian 37, 71–72
Mosquito aircraft **18**, **89**
  DH 98: 6, **6**, 7
  DZ695: 11, **11**
  DZ696: 11
  F II DZ695: 10–11, **11**, **46** (94)
  FB 40 A52-500/NA-A **56** (95)
  FB VI 9, 13, **13**, 26–27, **26**, 29, 30, **31**, **32**, **34**
  FB VI HJ719: **9**
  FB VI HJ770: 35
  FB VI HJ811: **12**, 13, **46** (94)
  FB VI HP867/OB-Z **48** (94)
  FB VI HP884: **91**
  FB VI HP886/UX-H **49** (94)
  FB VI HP939/OB-A **48** (94)
  FB VI HR374/OB-Z **50** (94)
  FB VI HR402/OB-C **42**, **51** (95), 60, **60**
  FB VI HR403/UX-B **51** (95)
  FB VI HR551/UX-P **54** (95)
  FB VI HR562/VE-T **56** (95)
  FB VI HR567: **52** (95), 76–78
  FB VI HX821/K **47** (94)
  FB VI RF582/VE-K **53** (95)
  FB VI RF700/KU-V **53** (95)
  FB VI RF711/A **55** (95)
  FB VI RF784/UX-N **68**
  FB VI TA477/UX-F **67**
  Mosquito HR526: **58**, 59
  PR 34 RG203/E **54** (95)
  PR IX 18–19, **47** (94)
  PR XVI 24, **24**, **49** (94), **50** (94), **55** (95)
Murray, Wg Cdr William Moffat 20, **20**, 23
Myers, F G 38–39, 41

Nakajima Ki-43 'Oscar' fighters 10, 11, 19, 57, 59, 60, 67
Nankervis, Flt Lt Jack **65**, 66
Newman, Sqn Ldr Kossuth 'Koss' Newman 23, **23**
Nicholls, Flg Off H M 'Nick' 42, **42**, 43, 60
Nicolson, Wg Cdr Eric James Brindley 'Nick' 26, 27, **27**, 89

Operation *Dracula* 81, 82, 83
Orsborn, Sgt Harold 'Ossie' 12–16, 27–28, 29, **29**, 31, 34, 57, 59, 62, 65–66, 71, 75, 76–78, 95

pilot training 26–27, 31
Pinkerton, WO Robert Conrie 'Pinky' **60**, 64, 66–67
Port Blair 20–21, **21**, 22
Pridmore, Sgt Alfred 'Alf ' 16–17, **17**, 23–24, **39**, 43–44, 75
prisoners of war **81**, 82–84

reconnaissance 11, 18–25
rhubarbing 29, 58–59, 64, 67, 69, 73, 83

Saunders, Wg Cdr Arthur 'Soapy' 63, 74, 76, **82**, 83, 86, 87
Shortis, Flt Sgt Jack 27, 29, 44, 95
Sittang Bend, Battle of the 89
Snell, Sqn Ldr 'Freddy' 38, 45, 63, 66, 71, 76
strike/intruder operations 11, 42–45, 57–92
  build-up 26–34
  January 1945: 58–63
  February 1945: 63–70
  March 1945: 70–76
  April 1945: 76–82
  May 1945: 82–86
  June 1945: 86–88
  July 1945: 88–91
  August 1945: 90–93
  Kumbhirgram 32–34, **43**
  operational sorties by squadron *93*
  psychological effects 66
Stumm, Wg Cdr Harley 30, 31, 36–37, 94

Taylor, Flg Off Bill 45, **45**, 57
Thewlis, Sgt Gordon 68–69, 82, 84
Thompson, Plt Off Tommy 68, 69–70, 83
Torrance, Flt Lt Alexander 'Jock' 27, 29–30, 32, 33, **34**, 42, 57, 62
Tuffnell, Flg Off William 'Tuffy' 37, **37**, 94

Walker, Wg Cdr Robert 'Johnny' **30**, 31, 32, 33, 34, 40, 43, 61, 63, 74–75
Walsh, Flt Sgt Benjamin 'Benny' 12–16, **14**, 27, **28**, 29–30, **29**, 31, 34, 57, 59–60, 62, **62**, 65–66, 71, 72, 75, 76–78, 95
Wambeek, Flg Off Ronald 'Babe' 37–38, 39–40, 59, 71–72
weapons
  anti-aircraft (AA) fire 22, 57, 60–61, 63
  atomic bombs 90
  bombs 9, 32, 42, 58, 62, 64, **65**, 70, 79
  cannon 9, 30, 32, 69
  machine guns 9, 33, 69
  Parafexes 65–66
Willis, Plt Off Bob 40, 68, 69–70, 73, 83, 86–87
Winship, Flg Off Jack 22–23

Yanota, Sgt Johnny 16, **16**, 28, 29, 42–43, 80, 82–84, 94